VIRGINIANS ALL

Virginians All

by Carlo Uchello
Illustrated by Marilyn Barr

PELICAN PUBLISHING COMPANY
GRETNA 1992

Copyright © 1992
By Pelican Publishing Company, Inc.
All rights reserved

The word "Pelican" and the depiction of a pelican are trademarks of Pelican Publishing Company, Inc., and are registered in the U.S. Patent and Trademark Office.

Library of Congress Cataloging-in-Publication Data

Uchello, Carlo.
   Virginians all / by Carlo Uchello ; illustrated by Marilyn Barr.
     p.   cm.
   Summary: Twenty-nine brief biographies of famous Virginians of the past and present, including athletes, entertainers, writers, politicians, military figures, and Native Americans.
   ISBN 0-88289-853-1
   1. Celebrities–Virginia–Biography–Juvenile literature.
[1. Virginia–Biography.]   I. Barr, Marilyn, ill.   II. Title.
CT265.U24   1992
920.0755–dc20
[B]   92-13634
                                                                                   CIP
                                                                                     AC

Manufactured in the United States of America

Published by Pelican Publishing Company, Inc.
1101 Monroe Street, Gretna, Louisiana 70053

*To Patsie,
without whom, nothing;*

and

*to Virginia and Jean-Pierre,
and all the sons and daughters
of the New Dominion*

CONTENTS

Introduction 9
Arthur Ashe, Jr. 13
Pearl Bailey 17
Richard E. Byrd 21
Willa Cather 25
Patsy Cline 29
Jerry Falwell 33
Ella Fitzgerald 39
Patrick Henry 43
"Stonewall" Jackson 49
Thomas Jefferson 55
Robert E. Lee 61
Meriwether Lewis and William Clark 67
James Madison 71
George Mason 77
Cyrus McCormick 81
James Monroe 85
Pocahontas 91
Chief Powhatan 97
Sir Walter Raleigh 103
Walter Reed 107
Bill ("Bojangles") Robinson 113
Secretariat 119
Capt. John Smith 123
William Styron 127
Booker T. Washington 131
George Washington 137
Martha Washington 143
Doug Wilder 149
Woodrow Wilson 155

INTRODUCTION

The history of Virginia is the history of its people. And Virginia has produced many of America's most famous leaders, explorers, entertainers, and athletes.

This book tells the stories of some of these notable citizens. But this book has not tried to tell the story of every important Virginian. Instead, these profiles attempt to give only a sampling of the great accomplishments of Virginians.

The people in this book do not fit any general descriptions. They are black and white, men and women. Some were born into wealthy or well-respected families, but many were not. Some achieved their fame at an early age, while others did not achieve fame until they were older.

But these men and women shared one thing in common. They all worked hard and made the most of their talents and abilities. They realized that it was up to them to achieve the things they wanted. Their efforts made their achievements possible.

Their efforts and achievements inspire us today. For it is through our own efforts that we will create the future for ourselves and for future generations of Virginians.

VIRGINIANS ALL

ARTHUR ASHE, JR.
(1943-Present)

... *Wimbledon champion*

ARTHUR ASHE, JR. grew up in Richmond at a time when blacks and whites lived segregated lives. Like every other black person, Arthur had to sit at the rear of buses. But in one respect, Arthur was lucky. His father was a park policeman for the city. The Ashe family was able to live in a house next to the tennis courts and pool at Brook Field Playground, where Arthur's father worked.

Arthur's cousin was able to trace their family's roots all the way back to 1735. In that year, the HMS *Doddington* carried a boatload of slaves from Africa to Portsmouth, Virginia. One of the slave girls on board, whose name was not recorded, was Arthur's earliest ancestor in America.

When Arthur was six years old, his mother died. Although the family's loss was tremendous, Arthur's father managed to raise his sons, Arthur and Johnny. He expected his children to do chores around the house. He wanted them to learn the value of hard work.

Arthur was a small, skinny boy. He was not big enough to play certain sports, but he wanted to learn to play tennis. He began playing when he was seven years old. Young Arthur was quick and he had a good serve. By the time Arthur was ten, he had already won many trophies. But in the early 1950s, there weren't many opportunities for black people to play tennis. Tennis was mostly a sport for wealthy white people. Most of the tennis courts were in clubs, and most clubs excluded black people.

But Arthur was able to get ahead. He travelled to Lynchburg, Virginia, for tennis camps with Walter

Johnson, a black doctor who worked hard to develop young talent. Arthur eventually won boys' singles titles four times.

Arthur and his coaches knew that he'd have to practice year-round for him to be a great player. But there were no indoor courts in Richmond where Arthur could play in the winter. He moved to St. Louis and lived with Richard Hudlin, who coached Arthur in his senior year of high school. That year, Arthur won the Junior Singles Indoor Tournament.

The University of California in Los Angeles (UCLA) offered Arthur a tennis scholarship to attend their school. UCLA was one of the best colleges in the country for tennis, so Arthur was excited to go there. He won the U.S. hard court singles championship in 1963, and he won the U.S. Clay Court singles title in 1967. The city of Richmond honored Arthur in 1966 by declaring an "Arthur Ashe Day," and the mayor presented Arthur with a plaque.

Arthur was on the Davis Cup team for eleven years, starting in 1963. Arthur also joined the ROTC on UCLA's campus, and after his graduation and training, he went on to coach tennis at West Point Academy.

In 1970, Arthur Ashe turned professional and was able to play in tournaments all over the world. He visited South Africa and played in a tournament there, but only after the government agreed to allow black spectators equal access to the matches. Over the next few years, Arthur won the Australian Open and the Stockholm Open, and several world championship tournaments in Italy and Spain. But he still had not won one of the major titles in tennis. Some people thought he couldn't win "the big one."

But in 1975, Arthur silenced his critics by winning the World Championship of Tennis title and the men's singles title at Wimbledon—the biggest prize in tennis.

He defeated Jimmy Connors, the great Swedish player Bjorn Borg, and many others to win these tournaments. Arthur had reached the pinnacle of his career. He was the first black man to win a major singles tennis championship. He had been the number-one-ranked player in the United States in 1968, and by 1979 he was still ranked fifth. But in 1979, at the age of thirty-six, Arthur Ashe had a heart attack and had heart bypass surgery. His professional tennis years were over, and he retired in 1980.

Arthur's retirement did not mean he was finished with tennis. He was captain of the U.S. Davis Cup team from 1981 to 1985, and he frequently gave tennis clinics for young people. He has been back to Virginia many times, visiting family members. He now lives with his wife in New York City.

PEARL BAILEY
(1918-1990)

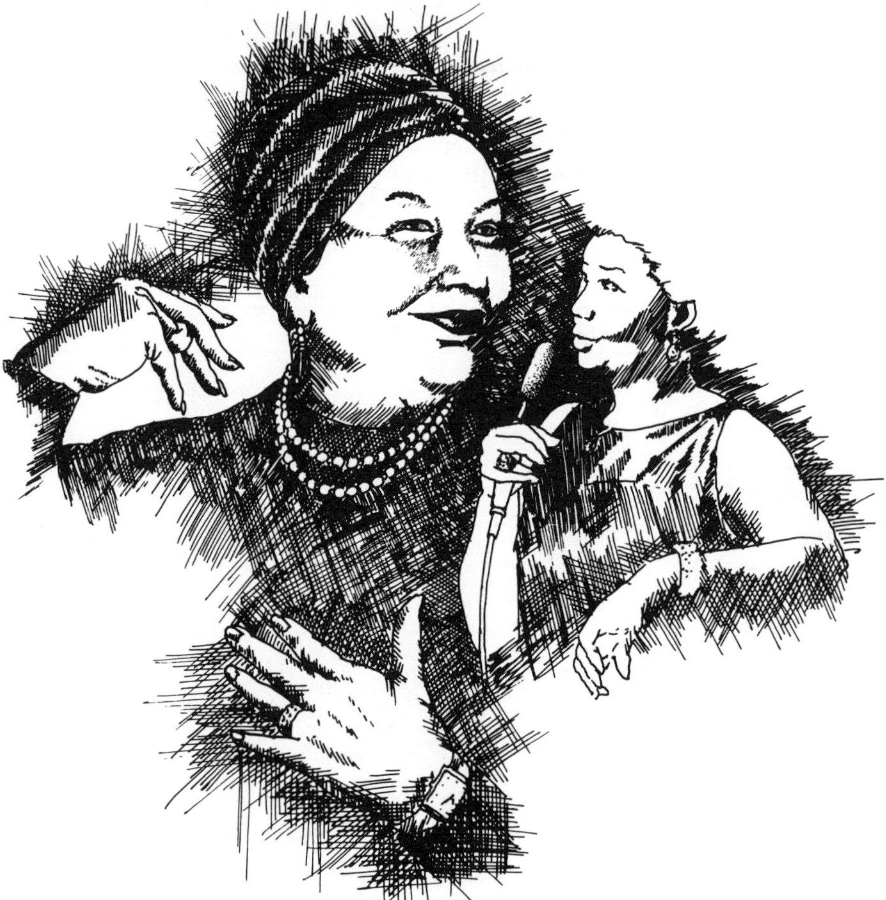

. . . "Aunt Pearl"

MILLIONS OF PEOPLE around the world knew Pearl Bailey as "Aunt Pearl," because she made them feel like they were a part of her family. Everyone who met her felt her love—her love of people and of life. Pearl Bailey was an exceptional singer and entertainer, but she was much more than that. She was everybody's favorite adopted aunt.

Like many black performers of her time, Pearl Bailey could trace her beginnings as a singer to her church choir. Her father was the Reverend Joseph James Bailey, and Pearl sang in her father's church from the age of three.

Pearl Bailey was born in Newport News, Virginia, in 1918. Her older brother, Willie, was a tap dancer and a protégé of Bill ("Bojangles") Robinson. The Bailey family moved to Washington, D.C., and when her parents separated later, Pearl alternated between Washington and Philadelphia.

It was through her brother's dancing that Pearl developed an interest in entertainment. Once, the theater where he was performing sponsored an amateur's contest. Pearl entered the contest, sang a few songs, and won, much to her brother's surprise. She was fifteen years old at the time.

Pearl accepted singing jobs whenever she could get them. For a while, she sang on U Street in Northwest Washington, an area that was known as "Black Broadway." She later worked in Pennsylvania coal-mine towns and made her way to New York. She got her big break in show business when she was asked to fill in for another performer who was sick. Soon she was singing at the Blue Angel club and at the famous Apollo Theater in Harlem.

"Pearlie Mae," as she was also known, joined a USO troupe during World War II, and entertained the servicemen overseas. When the war was over, she returned to singing in clubs. She was invited to join the cast of an all-black musical production, *St. Louis Woman*, on Broadway in New York, and then began her second career as an actress. She appeared in other plays and movies, including *Porgy and Bess* with Sammy Davis, Jr., and Sidney Poitier. But her biggest role was the lead in an all-black version of the musical *Hello, Dolly!* It opened at the National Theatre in Washington in 1967, and then went on to Broadway. Pearl received a Tony Award for her performance.

Pearl Bailey was a frequent performer in Las Vegas and other cities. By this time, she was widely known across the nation as a singer and actress. She had performed before presidents and other heads of state, and was a frequent guest at White House state dinners. In fact, she appeared there so often that she referred to it as "The House."

President Nixon named Pearl Bailey an "Ambassador of Love," and she was appointed to honorary positions with the American delegation at the United Nations. There, she made friends with representatives of many countries, who respected her for her sincerity and her concern for the people of the world. She was invited to visit many foreign countries, and she travelled widely with her husband (the drummer Louis Bellson) and their two adopted children. They toured refugee camps and hospitals, and also entertained kings and presidents around the world.

In 1978, Georgetown University in Washington invited Pearl Bailey to address the graduating class, and gave her an honorary degree. She had always regretted that she had not completed her education, so at the age of sixty, she entered Georgetown University as a college freshman. She continued her career as an entertainer, so it took her seven years to earn her degree. But at the age of sixty-seven, she earned her bachelor's degree in theology.

In 1988, she received two very special honors. Pres. Ronald Reagan awarded her the Medal of Freedom, the highest honor that a civilian can earn. And her hometown of Newport News opened a Pearl Bailey Branch Library in honor of her commitment to learning, and for encouraging others to resume their education.

Pearl Bailey died in 1990, just one week before she was scheduled to give an address at the United Nations, where she had served her country, and the world, so well.

RICHARD E. BYRD
(1888-1957)

...*polar explorer*

AS HE GREW UP in Winchester, Virginia, at the end of the nineteenth century, Richard Byrd dreamed of adventure. He had heard accounts of explorers who risked their lives while in the pursuit of new lands in the Arctic and in Africa. Some day, he thought, he would be the first man to reach the North Pole.

It was not meant to be. Richard was born too late, and he would soon read about Admiral Peary's adventures with a mixture of excitement and envy. He would have to find his own adventures elsewhere.

Richard managed to experience adventure at an early age, even by today's standards. He grew up as a member of a noted Virginia family, whose English roots went back to the seventeenth century in Virginia. His ancestors included William Byrd, who founded the cities of Richmond and Petersburg.

Richard's first adventure came at the age of twelve. A friend of the Byrd family, who was living in the Philippines, wrote to Richard and invited him for a visit. Without consulting his parents, Richard decided that he would go. Finally, Richard's parents agreed, although they were initially opposed to the idea of his travelling alone.

When the time came, Richard's mother took him to Washington, D.C., where he caught a train to San Francisco. He then boarded an ocean liner that took him to Japan, then Manila. On the way, the boat was caught in a terrible typhoon and almost sank.

After Richard arrived in the Philippines, he soon learned that a guerrilla war was being fought on the islands. This news only heightened his sense of adventure. He learned to carry and shoot a revolver, and he travelled as an observer with patrols that went into the interior of the islands to drive out the guerrilla soldiers.

Richard experienced many different things in the Philippines, and he realized that what he saw would be of interest to his family and neighbors in Virginia. He began writing letters to his family that were published in his hometown newspaper. These letters described Richard's experiences with the guerrilla war, but also other things he saw—spouting volcanoes, and the public hangings of captured guerrilla soldiers.

Soon, Richard was sent home when cholera broke out in the islands. His return voyage took him through the Indian Ocean, the Red Sea, the Mediterranean Sea, and the Atlantic Ocean. So, by the age of thirteen, young Richard had already travelled around the world!

Richard's enthusiasm for adventure was evident in everything he did. His education continued at the Shenandoah Military Academy and the University of Virginia. Then he went on to the U.S. Naval Academy, where he graduated in 1912—but only barely in the top half of his class. Richard was known more for his athletic abilities, where he excelled in football and gymnastics, in spite of several injuries.

After receiving his commission, Richard was stationed at the U.S. Naval Air Station in Pensacola, Florida. He learned to fly, and he served as a World War I pilot. After the war, he helped develop new navigational tools for aircraft and helped train Charles Lindbergh before his solo flight across the Atlantic Ocean.

In 1926, Richard Byrd and his pilot, Floyd Bennett, were the first men to fly over the North Pole. For this feat, he was awarded the U.S. Congressional Medal of Honor. Following his success at the North Pole, Byrd turn his sights southward. He organized an expedition to Antarctica and set up a base, Little America, in October 1928. The following year, Byrd and three others flew over the South Pole. In 1930, Byrd was promoted to rear admiral.

He organized three more expeditions to Little America. During the second expedition in 1934, Byrd spent five months alone in a shack at Advance Base, 123 miles south of Little America. Among the many items he took with him was some of his mother's Virginia ham!

While he was at Advance Base, he gathered scientific information about the weather and the atmosphere. Byrd expected to find peace in his self-imposed solitude, but he became very lonely, isolated as he was from humanity.

Byrd endured temperatures as low as eighty-four degrees below zero Fahrenheit while at Advance Base. A few months into his stay, fumes from a generator backed up and gave him carbon monoxide poisoning. He kept this a secret from his companions at Little America until they arrived, months later, to return him to base.

Byrd's successes made him an international hero. He served as an advisor to the Navy during World War II, and he wrote five books about his experiences as an explorer and Navy pilot. When Richard Byrd died in 1957, he was buried with full military honors at Arlington National Cemetery in Virginia.

WILLA CATHER
(1873-1947)

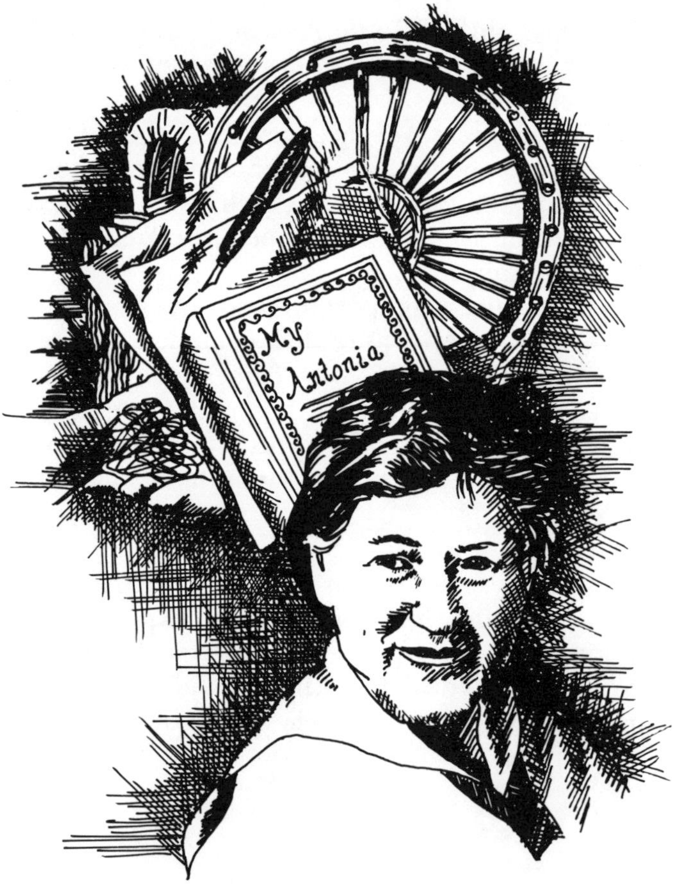
My
Antonia

. . . pioneer author

WILLA CATHER is not as popular today as she was earlier in this century, when she was considered to be one of the giants of American literature. But her work is still read and admired by a new generation of readers who enjoy her stories of settlers and frontier life in earlier times.

Willa Sibert Cather was born into a family that was torn apart by the Civil War. Willa's ancestors had been Irish and Welsh immigrants to America. Although both sides of her family were descended from early pioneer days in Virginia, her paternal grandfather had fought on the side of the Union in the Civil War. His house, which Willa used as the setting for one of her novels, had been used by the Union army as a field headquarters.

The resulting rift in the family was mended years later, but another one, of a different kind, was to develop. Willa's aunt and uncle moved from the family homestead in Virginia to Webster County, Nebraska. Many other persons from the East were moving to Nebraska and the new territories in the West, in search of large tracts of land. In a few years, Willa's grandparents followed suit and also left for Nebraska.

Willa loved the lush, green beauty of her Virginia home. She had been born in the Back Creek Valley area near Winchester in the Shenandoah Valley. The area of her birth is now known as Gore, Virginia. Willa's father was a sheep rancher who had decided to remain behind in Virginia. But in 1883, after the family's farm burned down, Willa's own family pulled up roots and followed the migration westward. They settled in Red Cloud, Nebraska, not far from the Kansas border.

Willa was struck by the sharp difference between her native Virginia and her new home. Nebraska was a dry, barren land of few trees, and not at all like her beloved Virginia.

Although she left Virginia at an early age, in a sense Willa Cather never really left her home. Later, when she began to write poetry, short stories, and novels, she returned to the people and places she had known in Virginia. Many of the houses and towns in her books were modelled after her own houses and towns, and many of the people in her books were modelled after family members and friends.

In spite of the differences between Nebraska and her native Virginia, Willa soon became acclimated to the rugged West. She was the oldest of seven children, and she was a very precocious child. She was interested in the many immigrants who had settled in Nebraska, and she tried to learn all she could about their countries, languages, and customs.

Willa became friends with the town doctor and enjoyed dissecting animals. When Willa went to the University of Nebraska, she planned a career in medicine. But a professor was so impressed with an essay she had written, that he secretly submitted it to a local newspaper. Willa was surprised and delighted to see her writing in print. She began studying theater and started writing for campus publications.

Shortly after her graduation, she left Red Cloud for Pittsburgh, where she became the editor of a Presbyterian family magazine called *The Home Monthly*. She continued to write poetry and short stories, and went on to write reviews of plays, operas, and books for the Pittsburgh *Leader* newspaper.

After a while, Willa Cather decided to become a high school teacher of Latin and English. She later sent a collection of her poetry to a publisher, who not only agreed to publish the work but who also offered her a job in New York City with his magazine. In two years, she became the magazine's managing editor.

Willa Cather continued to write fiction, using many of her experiences in her stories. Her two most famous novels, *O Pioneers!* and *My Antonia,* are stories of pioneers and immigrants and their lives on the farm in Nebraska. These novels tell the story of daily life on the farm and celebrate America as a great melting pot of nationalities. *My Antonia* includes a scene about a long train ride from Virginia to Nebraska. In 1923, Willa Cather won a Pulitzer Prize for her novel *One of Ours,* a story about a soldier in World War I.

Willa visited her home in Winchester, Virginia, in 1938 to reacquaint herself with the memories of her childhood. Her last novel, *Sapphira and the Slave Girl,* is set in Virginia, and is based on old stories from her childhood. Willa's grandfather's house, with its willow grove and spring, is the setting for the story.

Willa Cather was the first woman to receive an honorary degree from Princeton University. She was elected to the American Academy of Arts and Letters, and she received a gold medal from the National Institute of Arts and Letters. She died in 1947.

PATSY CLINE
(1932-1963)

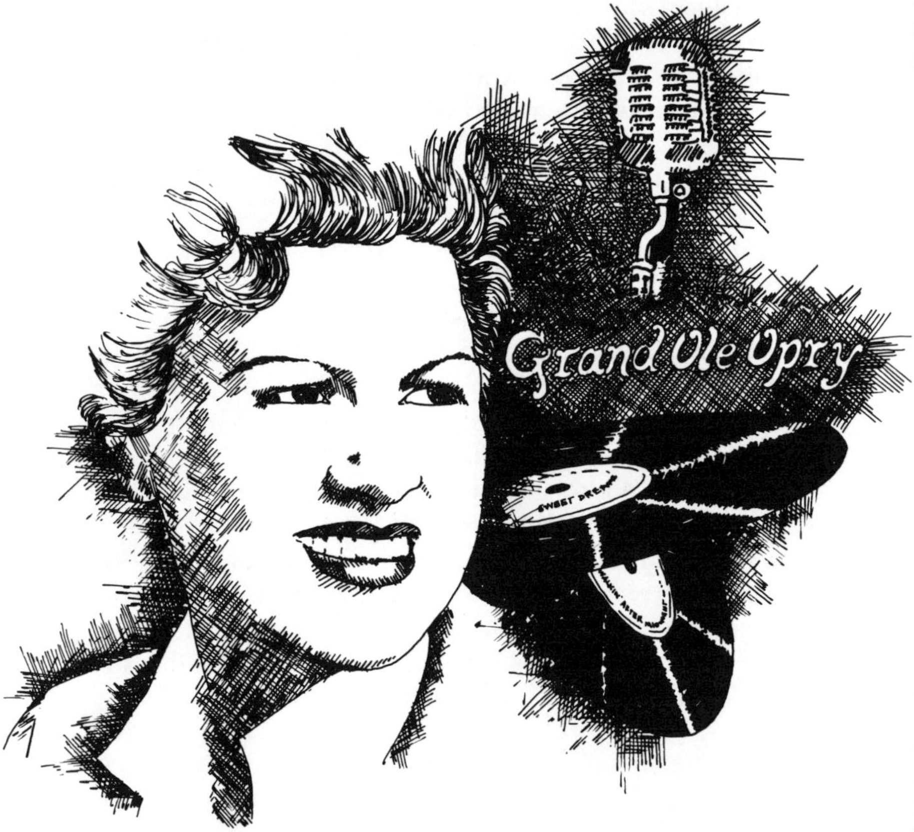
Grand Ole Opry

. . . country-western star

PATSY CLINE was born to be an entertainer. In the few short years before her tragic death, she became one of country music's most loved performers. And she was the first female country singer ever to gain popularity on the pop music charts.

Patsy Cline was born Virginia Patterson Hensley in Gore, Virginia, during the Great Depression. The Hensley family moved to Winchester, where little Virginia grew up. Early on, she showed a talent for performing. She won a tap dancing contest in Winchester when she was four years old. And although she couldn't read music, she learned to play the piano by ear when she was eight.

But in spite of her talent in dancing and playing the piano, Virginia Hensley soon showed an even stronger interest in singing. She sang at prayer meetings, in school musicals, and at weddings. Virginia believed in her own abilities long before anyone else recognized her as a talented singer. When she was sixteen, she bravely went to radio station WINC in Winchester and auditioned for a singing job. Soon, she was singing on the air with country musicians who came to town.

One of the musicians who came to town and sang with Virginia arranged for her to have an audition in Nashville at the Grand Ole Opry. She and her mother borrowed a friend's car and drove to Nashville. Virginia impressed them with her singing, but before they could offer her a job, her money ran out and she had to return to Winchester.

Virginia was forced to leave high school in her junior year. Her father abandoned the family, and

Virginia had to get a job to help support the family. She worked at a local drugstore in Winchester, but she kept on singing in her spare time. She sang with a local group, Bill Peer and the Melody Playboys, and she took the name Patsy Hensley. Patsy was a nickname for her middle name of Patterson.

Patsy Hensley sang in Winchester, Front Royal, and Charles Town. At one of her performances, she met Gerald Cline. They were married in 1953, and Patsy then became known to her audiences as Patsy Cline. But Patsy and her husband were not happy together, and their marriage lasted only a few years.

In 1956, Patsy went to the Town and Country Jamboree at Turner's Arena in Washington, D.C., and auditioned for a singing job. Soon, she was singing and sharing top billing with Jimmy Dean, who would also become a country music star.

But Patsy's big break came the next year, when she sang "Walkin' After Midnight" on Arthur Godfrey's "Talent Scouts" show. The audience stood and cheered when she finished her song. She won the competition, and a recording of the song was released. Selling over half a million copies, it reached number three on the *Billboard* magazine country music chart.

Patsy's personal life was changing for the better, too. In 1957, she married Charles Dick, from Winchester. She stopped singing for a while after the birth of their baby daughter. But she returned to the Grand Ole Opry at radio station WSM in Nashville in 1960. Now her professional career was ready to take off.

Patsy signed a recording contract with Decca Records, and soon recorded her number-one hit, "I Fall to Pieces." But soon afterwards, she was seriously injured in an automobile accident. For a while, the doctors didn't think she would live. She spent thirty-five days in the hospital, and when she left, she was confined to a wheelchair for several months.

Patsy returned to the Grand Ole Opry, and sang while standing on crutches. Soon, she was back in the recording studio, recording a song that was written for her by Willie Nelson. The song was "Crazy," and it, too, became a hit. She recorded it while still bandaged from her automobile accident.

More hit records followed. Patsy Cline and a group of other Grand Ole Opry stars sang before a sold-out house at Carnegie Hall in New York City. In 1960, Patsy was named the Top Female Artist of the Year by *Billboard* magazine. She performed in Las Vegas and at the Hollywood Bowl.

By 1963, Patsy Cline was at the peak of her success. She had released three albums and many hit records. She was friends with many country singers, and she helped several other performers get started in the business.

In March 1963, Patsy and many other country music performers went to Kansas City to perform at a benefit concert for a disk jockey who had died in an automobile accident. Patsy Cline, her manager, and two other performers were flying back to Nashville in bad weather when their plane crashed near Camden, Tennessee. All four people on board the small plane were killed. Patsy Cline was only thirty years old.

Patsy Cline was elected to the Country Music Hall of Fame in 1973. Many more albums of her songs were released after her death. And in 1985, a movie called *Sweet Dreams* was made about her life.

Patsy Cline's short life was filled with great triumph and great pain. Even today, many years after her death, she is still considered one of the greatest female country-western stars of all time.

JERRY FALWELL
(1933-Present)

. . . founder of Moral Majority

IN THE 1980s, it was virtually impossible to speak about religion or politics in America without mentioning the influence of Jerry Falwell. This small-town minister from Lynchburg, Virginia, emerged on the national scene as a spokesman for religious and conservative people across the nation, regardless of their denomination. He brought many people out of the shadows and into voting booths. As a measure of his influence and success, one pollster credited Jerry Falwell with the election of Ronald Reagan as president in 1980.

Depression-era rural Virginia seemed an unlikely place from which a national figure would arise. Jerry's father, Carey Falwell, owned a fleet of fuel trucks. He had many other businesses as well, including a dance hall and restaurants.

But Carey was a tormented man. Two years before Jerry was born, Carey killed his own younger brother in a duel. Although he acted in self-defense, Carey would never forgive himself for what he had done. He began to drink, and his drinking turned into alcoholism. In those days, there was not much help available to alcoholics or their families.

When Jerry and his brother, Gene, were born (they are twins, but not identical), there were already two older Falwell children, Virginia and Lewis. Another child, Rosha, had died of pneumonia.

Carey Falwell was not a religious person, but Jerry's mother, Helen Falwell, was. She made sure that her children were raised with religion. She liked to play radio broadcasts of preachers, both for herself and for her children.

Jerry Falwell had a reputation of being a practical joker, even early in school at Mountain View Elementary. He once locked a teacher in a closet so he could avoid taking a test! But Jerry was a good student, too. He graduated as valedictorian of Brookville High School in Lynchburg, a few years after his father died of alcoholism.

Jerry wanted to be an engineer, and he never paid much attention to religion. He entered Lynchburg College and was awarded the B. F. Goodrich Award for being the "Mathematics Student of the Year." When he was a sophomore, he agreed to attend a church service with a friend who had promised there would be pretty girls at church! He went to the service and was converted. (He also met Macel Pate, who would eventually become his wife in 1958.)

Jerry was an athlete in high school and college, playing both baseball and basketball. He even tried out for a professional baseball contract with the St. Louis Cardinals in 1952. But soon he was adding to his already busy schedule with many church-related activities. After his sophomore year, he decided to transfer to Baptist Bible College in Springfield, Missouri. He had not yet decided to become a preacher. But while he was there, he taught Sunday School classes. Just before his graduation as valedictorian, Jerry was asked to preach at a weekend church service while the pastor was away. He prayed and fasted for several days before he preached, and when he had finished, he knew that he would become a minister.

After graduation, Jerry Falwell returned to Lynchburg and the church where he was converted. Jerry found a church that was torn apart. The old pastor was gone, and many of the members wanted to organize a new church with Jerry as their pastor. After much prayer, Jerry agreed. They found a meeting place on Thomas Road that at one time had been a factory called the Donald Duck Bottling Company.

Jerry began recruiting new church members, going door to door at first, and then by preaching on a local radio station. Within one year, membership in the Thomas Road Baptist Church had grown from 35 members to 864 members. In the 1970s, Jerry turned to television, buying time on a local Lynchburg station. Soon the small church needed to be enlarged several times to hold their growing congregation.

The Falwell family was growing, too. Jerry and Macel had three children: Jerry, Jr., Jeannie, and Jonathan.

By 1969, the Thomas Road Baptist Church was the ninth largest church in America. Jerry Falwell and his fundamentalist message was getting noticed across America. In the early 1970s, he opened the Liberty Bible Institute and the Liberty Baptist Theological Seminary. Jerry Falwell was well on his way to reaching his dream of spreading the gospel to millions of people. His television ministry show, "The Old Time Gospel Hour," was carried by hundreds of stations across America. And his future as a minister might have gone unchanged, except for an event in 1973 that changed Jerry Falwell's life.

In that year, the U.S. Supreme Court voted to permit abortions during the first three months of pregnancy. Jerry Falwell and many other Americans were appalled. To them, this was nothing more than legalized baby killing. Until then, most fundamentalist preachers kept out of politics and instead focused on only the spiritual side of their congregations. But Jerry Falwell decided that the time had come to act.

He began to preach about the evils of abortion, and he told his church members about the decline of morality in America. Some people felt that Jerry

Falwell had no right to use his church as a forum for his political views. But the nation was ready for Jerry Falwell. Years of protest, often violent, against the American government had shattered many people's trust and faith in traditional institutions. Jerry Falwell represented a return to the basic American values of God and family.

Jerry Falwell preached for a return to traditional moral values and for a resurgence of patriotism. In 1976, he organized and staged a series of "I Love America" rallies across the nation to celebrate the Bicentennial. And in 1979, an organization called Moral Majority was begun, to organize and mobilize conservatives of all faiths into a powerful voting bloc. Their main political aims included supporting candidates who were opposed to both abortion and the Equal Rights Amendment for women, and who favored a return to prayer in the public school classrooms of America.

In 1980, Moral Majority contributed greatly to Ronald Reagan's election as president, and to the election of conservative congressmen across the nation. At its peak in 1984, Moral Majority boasted six and a half million members. By one poll, Jerry Falwell was the second most admired man in America, after President Reagan.

In the end, Moral Majority was overshadowed by other more activist anti-abortion groups. Moral Majority was dissolved in 1989, having claimed that it had achieved its objectives. And, in fact, it had been wildly successful. Jerry Falwell and Moral Majority had contributed to a new agenda in American politics. The election of Ronald Reagan, and later, of George Bush, gave conservatives the opportunity to appoint Supreme Court justices and other judges who shared their views. The influence of Jerry Falwell and Moral

Majority will continue to be felt across America for many years to come.

ELLA FITZGERALD
(1918-Present)

. . . world-famous jazz singer

MAYBE ELLA FITZGERALD was destined to become a famous singer. But on that amateur night at the Harlem Opera House in 1934, it was pure luck that she was up on stage, winning first prize. Ella and two of her girlfriends went to the theater on a dare. They drew straws to see which of them would go on stage and perform. Ella drew the short straw, so she had to perform.

Ella had planned to dance for her act, since she was a good tap dancer and she also knew most of the popular dances. But as she waited in the wings offstage, she saw that the act that was performing before her was a dance team that was well liked by the audience. She knew that she could not go on stage and dance right after another dancing act had finished. So, she changed her mind at the last minute and decided to sing.

Ella was sixteen years old, tall and skinny, very shy, and very unsure of herself. She started singing softly, and then her voice gained strength. The audience quickly started to pay attention. By the time she had finished, the audience was cheering for another song. When the amateur night was over, Ella had won the twenty-five-dollar first prize. But more importantly, she knew that she wanted to be an entertainer. She learned that she had a natural talent to entertain and perform, and the more she sang, the more confident she became.

Ella Fitzgerald was born in Newport News, Virginia. She never knew her real father, although she heard stories of how he had liked to play the guitar. Maybe he was able to pass along to his daughter the gift of music. He died soon after Ella was born. But Ella's mother also liked music, and she encouraged Ella to sing.

When Ella was young, she and her mother moved to New York. Ella's mother worked as a caterer and in a laundry. Ella attended school and sang in the school's glee club. She and her friends would often venture into Harlem, on the north end of Manhattan, where many black people lived. Most of the leading black artists, writers, and musicians lived in Harlem, and this period of black culture in the 1920s was known as the Harlem Renaissance.

In 1934, Ella auditioned for a job with a CBS radio show. She won the part, but before she could sign the contract, her mother died. Ella had to abandon the show before she could even begin it, because she was still a minor and she had no legal guardian. She lived for a while with an aunt, and later in an orphanage. But she also kept singing in amateur-night contests. Finally her hard work began to pay off and she was offered a job with the Harlem Opera House. She performed for the first time in 1935. And even then, she had to lie about her age so she wouldn't be considered a minor.

During one of her performances, she was spotted by a member of the Chick Webb Orchestra. Chick Webb was a jazz drummer who had started his own band when he was seventeen. It was arranged for Ella to sing for him, and he decided to give her a chance. She sang before a crowd at Yale University and impressed them so much that Chick Webb hired her to sing with his band.

Ella Fitzgerald sang with Chick Webb's band in ballrooms, and she made recordings with the group. She sang for live radio broadcasts, where she earned a national reputation. She was the first female singer to develop a jazz-style voice.

Her first big hit, which she co-wrote, was a jazz recording of the nursery rhyme "A-Tisket, A-Tasket." It was one of the most popular songs of the 1930s. By 1943, Ella had written lyrics to enough songs that she became the youngest person ever to become a member of the American Society of Composers, Authors, and Publishers.

Ella sang with Chick Webb's band until he died in 1939. Then, the band continued for a while under a new name: Ella Fitzgerald and Her Orchestra. She began singing in a wide variety of styles—jazz, bebop, calypso, Broadway show tunes, and popular songs. Her voice was recognized for having a wide range and an incredible sweetness. But Ella Fitzgerald became even more famous for her "scat" singing. In scat singing, she would sing nonsense words or sounds in the place of lyrics, to imitate the sound of a musical instrument.

Later, she would become part of a group of musicians known as Jazz at the Philharmonic. Ella Fitzgerald recorded and performed worldwide with other great jazz and blues musicians, such as Dizzy Gillespie. She has recorded albums of songs by America's top composers, such as George Gershwin, Irving Berlin, Cole Porter, Duke Ellington, and others.

Ella Fitzgerald has received many honors. For eighteen years in a row, she won *Down Beat* magazine's award for "Best Female Jazz Singer." She received Kennedy Center Honors in Washington, D.C., for her lifetime achievement in the performing arts, and received the National Medal of Arts in 1987. Ella Fitzgerald continues to please audiences wherever she performs.

PATRICK HENRY
(1736-1799)

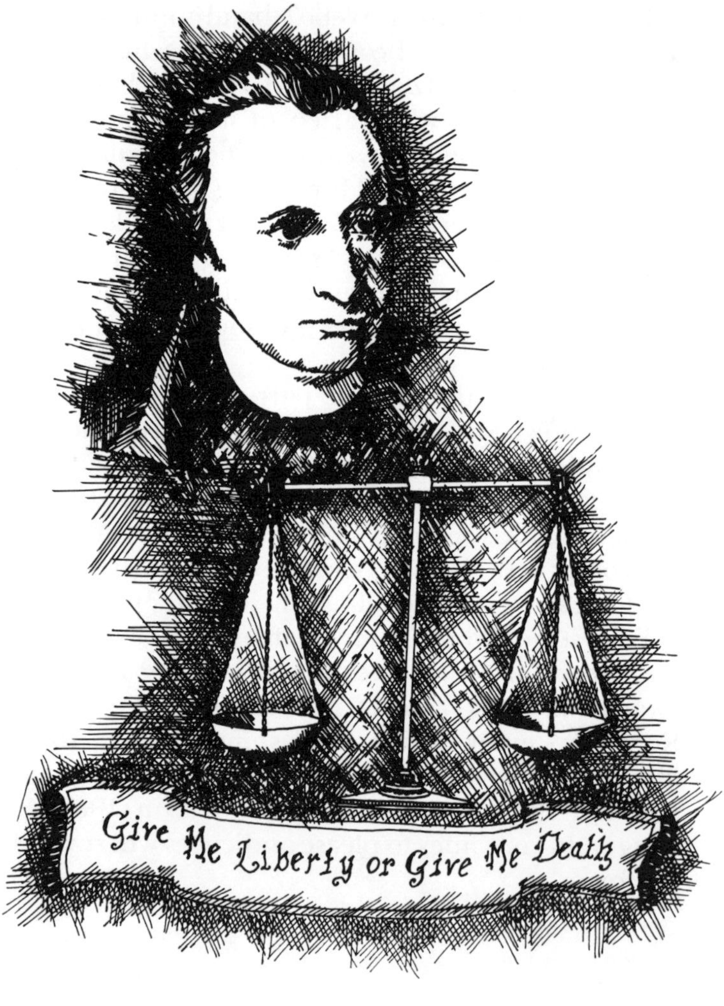
Give Me Liberty or Give Me Death

. . . *a man of the people*

JOHN HENRY was a college-educated man from Scotland who moved to Virginia and raised his family. He owned land and was well respected in Hanover County. But he had no real prospects for wealth. Since he could not afford to send his son, Patrick, away to school, he taught his son Latin, Greek, mathematics, and history at home.

Young Patrick was a naturally curious boy who loved music and nature. He taught himself how to play the violin, flute, lute, and harpsichord.

Patrick also had an uncle who lived in a cabin in the mountains. Patrick loved visiting his uncle, who took him along on hunting and fishing trips.

Although his father was an Episcopalian, Patrick's mother took him with her to hear Presbyterian ministers who travelled across Virginia. Many of the Presbyterian ministers were dynamic speakers who excited their audiences. Patrick was impressed by their speaking abilities. Patrick remained an Episcopalian all his life, but he was always tolerant of other people's religious beliefs.

When he was fifteen, Patrick Henry went to work as a clerk in a country store. The following year, John Henry helped his sons Patrick and William open a small general store. But in less than a year, the store went bankrupt. Patrick took to farming, then married Sarah Shelton in 1754. Her father was a farmer who also owned a tavern across from the Hanover courthouse.

When Patrick and Sarah married, her father gave them 300 acres of land as a wedding present. The young couple started a tobacco farm, but the land was not very good and their crops were never very successful. After a few years of drought, Patrick decided that he had to do something different. At his father-in-law's tavern, he had heard lawyers talking about their cases, and Patrick was very curious about the strange legal terms that lawyers used.

Since he could not afford to travel to London for his legal training, Patrick obtained law textbooks and taught himself. In less than six months, he took his examinations and passed.

In the courtroom, Patrick remembered how, in his youth, the Presbyterian ministers were able to use their voices to influence their audiences. Patrick quickly learned to speak in a way that convinced juries of his arguments. He became popular for defending the rights of common people against authority figures. Patrick Henry was soon elected to the House of Burgesses in Williamsburg.

At that time, the English king, George the Third, appointed governors in the American colonies. The English Parliament passed laws that taxed the colonies and limited their self-control. Led by Patrick Henry, the House of Burgesses passed resolutions that challenged the English Parliament. The Americans wanted to be treated fairly by the English, so they protested the English taxes by refusing to buy some English goods. In Boston, some Americans dumped a boatload of tea into the water to protest the tax.

Patrick Henry led the fight in Virginia for American independence. All thirteen colonies agreed to send representatives to Philadelphia so that America would speak with one voice. Patrick was a delegate from Virginia to both Continental Congresses in Philadelphia.

Some of the delegates were afraid of provoking the English into a war. Patrick Henry stood up to speak.

He argued that war with England was inevitable and the colonies should prepare for it. He told the assembly, "Is life so dear, or peace so sweet, as to be purchased at the price of chains and slavery? Forbid it, Almighty God! I know not what course others may take; but as for me—give me liberty or give me death!"

Patrick's words spread throughout the colonies. Preparations were made for war, and "Liberty or Death!" became the battle cry. Patrick was elected colonel of the First Virginia Regiment. Later, after the Declaration of Independence was signed, Patrick Henry was elected as Virginia's first American governor.

As governor, Patrick Henry helped the American war effort by sending troops and supplies to Gen. George Washington. It was a long, hard war, but at last the Americans were victorious. During the war, Patrick had served for five one-year terms as governor, and in the Virginia state legislature. Now he was called upon to help with the new American Constitution.

Patrick Henry never forgot the common people. He believed that the new constitution did not protect people enough, so he fought to amend the constitution. The first ten amendments to the constitution, known as the Bill of Rights, were passed to protect people from the powers of a large, central government.

Patrick returned to his life as a simple lawyer and farmer. Years later, people thought about asking him to run for president of the United States. George Washington tried to convince Patrick Henry to become secretary of state or chief justice of the Supreme Court. But Patrick wasn't interested. He had already dedicated most of his life to his country, and he wanted a quiet life.

Finally, Patrick agreed to return to the Virginia legislature. Before he could begin his term in

Richmond, he died of cancer. He was sixty-three years old.

Patrick Henry's words and actions inspired the American Revolution. He convinced the other colonies that they could defeat England by working together. Years earlier, he had told them, "The distinctions between Virginians, Pennsylvanians, New Yorkers, and New Englanders are no more. I am not a Virginian, but an American."

"STONEWALL" JACKSON
(1824-1863)

... Civil War hero

MANY HISTORIANS BELIEVE that when "Stonewall" Jackson died in 1863, the South's chances of victory in the Civil War died with him. Certainly his war record was unequaled: in twenty-five months of leading his rebel troops, he never suffered a single defeat. If he had lived, and if the South had followed his strategy, the South might have captured Washington, D.C. and won the war.

Stonewall Jackson did not want war, and he did not want the South to leave the Union. But when war broke out, he volunteered his services and commanded the Confederate troops from Virginia.

Thomas Jonathan ("Stonewall") Jackson was born to Jonathan and Julia Jackson in Clarksburg, Virginia (now a part of West Virginia), one of four children. The Jackson family had its roots in England and Ireland, and they had become prosperous. Thomas's grandfather, Edward Jackson, was a successful land surveyor who invested in real estate. When he died, he left a sizeable fortune to each of his fifteen children.

His son Jonathan, Thomas's father, was a lawyer. By all appearances, he too was successful. But the truth was that he had made many bad loans and was nearly bankrupt. When Thomas was two years old, his father and sister died of typhoid fever. Thomas's mother soon learned that they were penniless. She earned some money by sewing and teaching, but she died five years later, when Thomas was seven. At this early age, Thomas was sent to live with an uncle at Jackson's Mill.

Thomas and his older brother, Warren, did not like going to school, and they ran away from home. They went to Ohio, then floated on a raft down the Ohio River. Thomas was only nine years old at the time! They eventually returned to their uncle's house and went to school.

As a young man, Thomas worked for a while as a constable, and one of his jobs was to collect debts. Perhaps it was because of his duties as a constable that Thomas became known as an exceptionally honest man. He worked hard, and in 1842 he received an appointment to West Point Academy. Although he had only a small amount of formal education, Thomas applied himself and was able to graduate seventeenth in his class.

After graduation, Thomas was sent to Mexico as a second lieutenant, to fight in the Mexican War. He displayed true leadership qualities and bravery in the face of great danger, and he was promoted to first lieutenant. While he was in Mexico he met Robert E. Lee, and he also met other soldiers who would one day fight on the Union side in the Civil War.

When the Mexican War ended, Thomas received orders to remain in Mexico as part of the occupation forces. But soon he grew tired of his peacetime assignment, and he resigned from the Army. He returned to Virginia in 1851 and became a professor of artillery tactics and natural philosophy (what we now call general science) at the Virginia Military Institute (VMI). Although he was well suited to teaching artillery tactics, his own lack of education in the sciences meant that he had to read and study the course materials each night before he could teach the next day! He was not a very popular or well-liked professor at VMI.

He married while at VMI, but a little over a year later, his wife and infant daughter died. Three years later, he married again, to Mary Anna Morrison, a minister's daughter.

When war broke out between the states in 1861, Thomas Jackson volunteered his services to the state of Virginia. He was commissioned a colonel in the Virginia Army and immediately organized the volunteers into a strong fighting brigade.

In his first major battle of the war, he was ordered to unite his troops with Gen. P. G. T. Beauregard's troops at Manassas, Virginia, to prevent the invasion of Union troops. Many people from Washington, D.C. rode out near the battleground in their fancy carriages, hoping to watch the Union army crush the rebel forces. But they and the Union troops had to beat a hasty retreat when the rebels defeated the Union army. In this First Battle of Manassas, also known as Bull Run, Thomas Jackson earned the nickname of "Stonewall." He positioned his troops into a strong defensive line, or wall, and withstood the Union army's attack. "Stonewall" Jackson's victory at Manassas made him a hero and a household name throughout the South.

The legend around Stonewall Jackson began to grow with each victory. He was a very secretive leader who kept his battle plans from his own officers until the last possible moment. He also had some habits that people considered odd. He always sat as straight as possible, whether in a chair or on horseback. And he seemed always to have a supply of lemons that he would suck constantly, throughout the war. No one knows where and how he got his supply of lemons.

Jackson's chain of victories included the Seven Days' Battles around Richmond, Harpers Ferry, Fredericksburg, and finally at Chancellorsville, Virginia. But the victory at Chancellorsville was won at a great cost to the South. While returning from the battle, Jackson was accidently shot by his own men. His wounds were not mortal, but he had to have his left arm amputated. When news of this reached Gen.

Robert E. Lee, he said, "He has lost his left arm, but I have lost my right arm." General Lee meant that he relied on Stonewall Jackson more than any of his other generals.

While recovering from his wounds, pneumonia set in, and Stonewall Jackson was dead within a week. He was only thirty-nine years old.

Stonewall Jackson was a complex man. For a Southern man and Confederate general, his views of black people were somewhat strange. He was not opposed to slavery, but he believed that black people should have formal religious training. In 1855, he founded a Colored Sunday School at his all-white church, and he contributed to it regularly. The day after the First Battle of Manassas, he took time from his duties to write to the pastor of his church, enclosing his contribution for the Sunday School.

THOMAS JEFFERSON
(1743-1826)

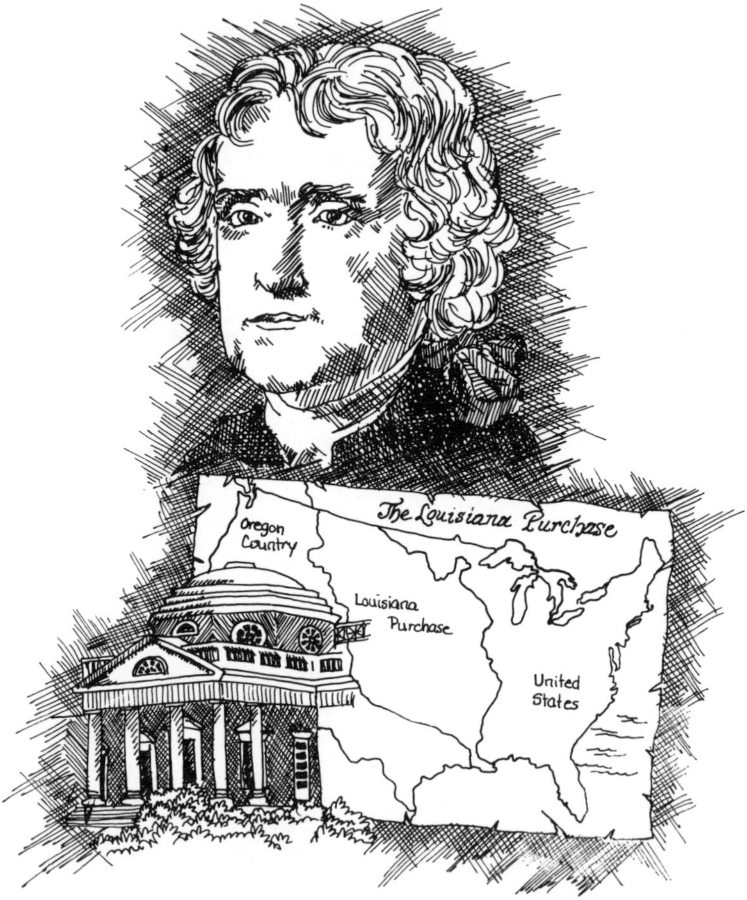
The Louisiana Purchase
Oregon Country
Louisiana Purchase
United States

. . . America's scholar-president

THOMAS JEFFERSON'S greatest gift to the United States and the world was the Declaration of Independence. It unified the thirteen colonies around a common statement of beliefs in their struggle against Great Britain. In the years since the American Revolution, it has inspired many other people and countries in their fights against oppression. But the Declaration of Independence was only one of the gifts that Thomas Jefferson gave to his country.

Thomas Jefferson was skilled in many things. He was a talented writer and lawyer, but he was also a farmer, a musician, an inventor, an architect, a mathematician, and a linguist!

His childhood and upbringing did not offer any clues about his eventual success and fame, though. Thomas was born in Shadwell, Virginia, about five miles east of Charlottesville. His father, Peter Jefferson, was a farmer and a surveyor. He was Welsh, and Thomas's mother was English and Scottish. Thomas was the third child in his family, and the older of two boys. When Thomas was two, his family moved to Tuckahoe, Virginia, to live on a relative's plantation. Later in his life, Thomas said that his earliest memory was the time when he was carried by a slave to Tuckahoe. Not many people can remember things from when they were two years old!

The Jefferson family moved back to Shadwell when Thomas was nine. Thomas received his education from tutors, but he realized very early that not everyone was as lucky as he was. He had played with slave children on the plantation, but he saw that they were never allowed to go to school. Thomas thought this was very wrong.

When Thomas was fourteen, his father died. As the older son, it was his responsibility to keep the family's farm operating. But Thomas's father had made sure that Thomas wouldn't have to quit school. He wanted his son to make his own decisions about his education and his future.

Thomas grew up to be a tall, muscular man. He was six feet, two and a half inches tall and had reddish hair. He had a fair complexion that was easily sunburned. When the time came for him to receive his higher education, he went to the College of William and Mary in Williamsburg, which was then the capital of Virginia. Thomas was excited about being in the big city.

He spent almost all of his time reading and studying, since he was interested in so many things. His professors introduced him to the royal governor of Virginia, and when Thomas left college, he decided to become a lawyer. He began practicing law in 1767.

Thomas practiced law and took care of his family's lands. He had inherited 2,500 acres of land when he was twenty-one. Thomas married Martha Wayles Skelton in 1772, and when her father died several years later, they inherited her family's estate.

Thomas was elected to the Virginia legislative assembly from 1769 to 1775. These years were very difficult for the American colonies. The British government increased taxes on the colonies, but they would not let the colonists govern themselves. Thomas wrote *A Summary View of the Rights of British America,* in which he stated that the British Parliament had no right to rule the American colonies.

In 1776, Thomas was a member of the Continental Congress in Philadelphia. The other representatives gave Thomas the job of writing the Declaration of

Independence. Even though several other people were more powerful and experienced, they realized that Thomas was the best writer. He wrote the first draft of the Declaration of Independence in a few days. Thomas was only thirty-three years old at the time.

After the colonists declared their independence from Great Britain, Thomas Jefferson was elected governor of Virginia and served from 1779 to 1781. Thomas was a good governor, and he fought hard to allow freedom of religious worship in Virginia. He also proposed a public school system so that everyone in Virginia could receive a good education.

Thomas Jefferson's most daring act as governor was to propose the abolition of slavery. Although he owned slaves, he knew that it was wrong to buy and sell other people. His attempt to end slavery was not successful, but some people began to see that Thomas was right about ending slavery.

The year 1782 was a sad one for Thomas. His wife, Martha, died after giving birth to their sixth child. Thomas never remarried, and he remained close to his children for the rest of his life.

Thomas served as America's minister to France from 1785 to 1789. Thomas lived in Europe for five years, but he returned to become America's first secretary of state under Pres. George Washington. He was elected vice-president in 1796, and he was elected the third president of the United States in 1800. He was the first president to take office in the new capital city of Washington, D.C.

Thomas Jefferson was a popular president. He believed strongly in the rights of the individual, and he fought against a big, centralized government. He was a spokesman for poor people who owned little or no land. He approved the Louisiana Purchase, which almost doubled the size of the United States. The United States paid only $15 million to France, or less than three cents an acre! Thomas Jefferson also supported the famous Lewis and Clark expedition into the new territory, and he founded the Library of Congress in Washington.

Thomas Jefferson could have been elected to a third term as president, but he decided that two terms were enough. He retired to his home at Monticello, which he designed, near Charlottesville. He also designed the new state capitol building in Richmond.

Later in his life, Thomas Jefferson was able to succeed in one of his greatest plans. He founded the University of Virginia in 1819, and raised money for its construction. He also designed most of the buildings for the university. Thomas was especially proud that he was responsible for creating a public university in Virginia.

Thomas Jefferson died on July 4, 1826, exactly fifty years after the signing of the Declaration of Independence. But his legacy lives on, in the institutions he created, and in the principles for which he stood. His belief in freedom and his belief in the rights of all people are the basis for our liberty today as American citizens.

ROBERT E. LEE
(1807-1870)

... the Virginia gentleman

IT IS NO small wonder that Robert E. Lee is revered, even today, throughout the South. He was so much more than the commander of the Confederate army in the Civil War, although that achievement was enough to earn him fame. Robert E. Lee was in many ways the perfect Virginia gentleman, and his wide fame is the result of his lifetime of service to his native Virginia and his country.

Robert E. Lee was born into a well-respected and notable Virginia family that had fallen on very hard times. Robert's father, "Light Horse Harry" Lee, was a hero of the American Revolutionary War, who later served as governor of Virginia and as a United States congressman. But for all of his accomplishments, "Light Horse Harry" Lee's fortunes turned to ruin. He loaned money that was never repaid, his crops failed, and he made a number of bad investments. He spent time in debtor's prison, and his family's wealth was gradually spent. Partly out of bad health and partly to avoid creditors, "Light Horse Harry" Lee left Virginia for the island of Barbados when Robert was only six years old. He died five years later, never having returned to Virginia.

But Robert E. Lee had memories of an earlier time. He had been born at Stratford Hall in the Northern Neck of Virginia, and he spent his early childhood there. No doubt he heard stories about his famous English ancestors, two of whom were signers of the Declaration of Independence. But because Robert's father did not own Stratford Hall, he and his family eventually had to move away. They settled in

Alexandria, Virginia. Robert learned to hunt and fish, and he swam in the Potomac River. He loved to go to horse markets, where he learned a lot about horses and how to tell if they were good. It was a skill that he was able to use years later, as a cavalryman and as a general.

He attended a school that was owned by one of his aunts in Fauquier County, and he showed a great aptitude for mathematics. Robert had decided to become a soldier like his father, so he applied to West Point Academy in New York. This was his only opportunity for a free college education. While he was a cadet there, he met many of the men who would fight on both sides of the Civil War. And Robert had a perfect conduct record, as he never received a single demerit while he was there.

Robert E. Lee graduated second in his class from West Point, and he was assigned to Fort Pulaski on the Savannah River, and then to Fort Monroe in Virginia. In 1831, the young Army lieutenant married Mary Anne Custis of Arlington. She was the only child of George Washington Parke Custis, who was a grandson of Martha Washington's from her first marriage. Robert and Mary lived for a while at Fort Monroe, and then Robert was transferred back to Washington as an assistant to the chief of engineers. They lived with Mary's parents at Arlington House, until Robert served in St. Louis, North Carolina, and New York while working on engineering projects.

At the age of thirty-nine, Robert E. Lee had never seen battle. But that changed when the United States declared war on Mexico in 1846. Lee distinguished himself during the war, and when he returned to Washington, he was appointed to the post of superintendent of West Point Academy. In his years there, he improved both the facilities and the curriculum of the academy.

When he left the academy, Lee was transferred to a cavalry regiment, and once again he served in the West. In 1859, while back at Arlington, he was called upon to put down an insurrection at Harpers Ferry that was being led by the abolitionist John Brown. John Brown had wanted to lead an armed revolt of slaves against their masters. Lee's Union army troops stormed the armory building where John Brown and his followers were staying. They captured John Brown, and he was later hanged.

But the issue of slavery did not die with John Brown. Two years later, Southern states began to secede from the Union. Robert E. Lee was offered the command of the Union army to put down the rebellion in the South. Although Robert E. Lee opposed slavery, he felt an obligation to defend his native Virginia. As he saw it, his home state was being invaded by a hostile force, and it was his responsibility to help defend it. He decided that he could not take up arms against his family, friends, and neighbors. He resigned his commission in the U.S. Army and joined the Confederate forces.

Lee led the Army of Northern Virginia into battle to defend the Confederate capital of Richmond. The Union had hoped to win the war in a few weeks or months, but Lee's brilliant strategy forced the Union to retreat after several important battles.

During the first few years of the war, Lee's army was wildly successful, and Lee was acknowledged as the greatest general of the war—on either side. But the South was at a great disadvantage, both in the number of troops and in the amount of material and food it had to support the troops. The Union army eventually wore down the South, which became unable to defend itself. In 1865, Robert E. Lee surrendered at Appomattox Court House to Gen. Ulysses S. Grant, who would eventually become president of the United States.

After the war, Robert E. Lee was offered the job of president of Washington College in Lexington, Virginia. Lee believed that education was essential for the South to recover from the effects of the war. Because of his reputation and hard work, the school prospered, and the enrollment at Washington College almost tripled in Lee's first year there. He remained at Washington College as president until he died.

In 1867, some people thought that Robert E. Lee should become governor of Virginia. A New York newspaper suggested that Lee should run for president of the United States against Ulysses S. Grant! Robert E. Lee wanted a quiet life, but wherever he went, he attracted attention. His fame increased for the remainder of his life.

Robert E. Lee died in 1870, and in the following year the trustees of Washington College voted to change the name of the college to Washington and Lee College.

In the years since his death, Robert E. Lee's reputation has grown even more. Many historians regard him as the greatest American general of all time. But as great a general as he was, it is a pity that many of his other accomplishments have been overshadowed. Robert E. Lee's whole life was one of service to his native state of Virginia and the United States.

MERIWETHER LEWIS
(1774-1809)

WILLIAM CLARK
(1770-1838)

. . . explorers of the Louisiana Territory

THE LEWIS AND CLARK EXPEDITION to the Pacific Northwest began with a small party of soldiers and guides, but ended with fame and honor for its two leaders, Meriwether Lewis and William Clark, both from Virginia.

Pres. Thomas Jefferson had purchased the Louisiana Territory from France in 1803. The United States paid France only $15 million, or less than three cents per acre, for the new territory. President Jefferson immediately decided to send out an exploring party to survey and take measure of the largely unexplored lands. He chose Meriwether Lewis, who was an old friend and a veteran of the Indian Wars, to lead the expedition. Meriwether Lewis chose his friend William Clark to join him on the expedition.

Jefferson wanted Lewis and Clark to discover a river route through the new territory to the Pacific Ocean. This route, if it could be found, would enable trading to take place more easily. Jefferson's instructions to Lewis and Clark were simple and direct. He wanted them to explore the Missouri River and its tributaries. He also wanted Lewis and Clark to identify and record information about the Indian nations, plant and animal life, climate, and geography of the territory. The U.S. Congress approved $2,500 to pay for the expedition.

Meriwether Lewis was born in Albemarle County in Virginia, near Charlottesville. His parents were of Welsh and English heritage. Meriwether's father had been an officer in the Revolutionary War, and had died when Meriwether was only five years old.

Meriwether was the older of two boys. He loved the wilderness, and he became an expert hunter at an early age. He went to school until he was eighteen, then volunteered for the militia. While he was on duty, he met William Clark, who was in charge of a company of sharpshooters. They became good friends.

William Clark was born in Caroline County, Virginia, four years before Meriwether Lewis. He was the younger brother of Gen. George Rogers Clark, who fought in the Revolutionary War. William had also joined the militia and fought in the Indian Wars.

When Thomas Jefferson became president in 1801, he asked his friend Meriwether Lewis to be his confidential White House secretary. Meriwether served his friend in this job until 1803.

Then, when President Jefferson offered him the chance to lead the expedition westward to the Pacific, Lewis eagerly accepted. He asked his friend William Clark to join him. William Clark's primary job would be to record what they saw, and to make maps.

The expedition set off from St. Louis in May 1804, with a party of about twenty-five soldiers, guides, and interpreters. They used canoes to travel up the Missouri River deep into Indian territory. When they reached what is now North Dakota, they were joined by Sacajawea (a sixteen-year-old Indian girl), her French-Canadian husband, and their baby son. Sacajawea was the sister of the Shoshone Indian chief, and she could interpret for the travellers. She stayed with Lewis and Clark for about eighteen months, until they reached Three Forks, Montana.

Lewis and Clark travelled across the Rocky Mountains by horse, and then canoed on the Snake and Columbia rivers to the Pacific Ocean. They did not find a direct river route to the ocean from St. Louis, but when they returned, they had compiled a valuable inventory of the people, animal life, and geography of the new territory.

Meriwether Lewis was a brave and intelligent expedition leader. William Clark proved to be an excellent map-maker, and he was able to establish good relations with the Indians. He also created many detailed drawings of the animals that they observed.

The whole expedition covered over 6,000 miles. On the return voyage, Meriwether Lewis was almost killed by Blackfoot Indians. Later, he was accidently shot during a hunting expedition, but he recovered. The expedition, when it ended, had lasted almost two and a half years.

Once the expedition was over, Lewis and Clark each received 1,600 acres of land as a reward for their hard work. President Jefferson appointed Meriwether Lewis to the position of governor of the Missouri Territory. He served in that post until his death.

William Clark was placed in charge of the militia and supervised America's relations with the Indians of the Missouri Territory. He was later governor of the Missouri Territory for eight years. He was trusted by the Indians and helped to avoid war with them, keeping the peace on the frontier.

Lewis and Clark's voyage of discovery made it possible for thousands of settlers to move westward and expand the borders of the young American nation.

JAMES MADISON
(1751-1836)

...father of the Constitution

JAMES MADISON was a small man. He was only five feet, six inches tall, and very slightly built. But he was a giant among men, one of the founding fathers of the American nation. Through his leadership, the U.S. Constitution was written and ratified by the states, and the Bill of Rights was approved by Congress. George Washington was the "Father of His Country," but James Madison was known as the "Father of the Constitution."

James' early life was a quiet one, and typical of English boys who grew up in the colonies in the eighteenth century. He was born in his grandmother's house in King George County, Virginia, and he was the oldest son of James and Eleanor Conway Madison. But his father owned property in Orange County near the Blue Ridge Mountains, and at the age of nine, James and his family moved there. James' father named their house Montpelier, and James would spend most of his life there.

As a young boy, James was very shy and soft-spoken. His education came mostly from tutors, and when the time came for him to go to college, he chose Princeton in New Jersey. He and his tutor rode on horseback to Princeton, and they passed through Philadelphia, which was then the largest city in the colonies. James was fascinated by what he saw. And when James arrived at Princeton, he put all of his efforts into his work. He finished his four year program in only two years, but he worked so hard that he became very sick.

After graduating from Princeton, James studied theology and Hebrew for a year, and then returned to

Montpelier to study law at home. He had become excited about the growing talk of independence in the colonies, and he wanted to serve Virginia as a representative. He bought 200 acres of land from his father, so he could vote and run for public office, since that was a requirement. And he spoke early for full independence from Great Britain.

He was elected to the Virginia Constitutional Convention in 1776, and the Continental Congress in 1780. By 1781, the United States had won its war of independence, but it didn't have a real government. Between 1776 and 1788, there was no president and no constitution, only the Articles of Confederation. But instead of uniting the thirteen colonies into one nation, the Articles allowed the states to make their own laws, and to worry only about what was best for them individually.

James Madison knew that the thirteen states needed a strong government, and strong laws. He helped organize the Constitutional Convention in 1787, which produced the American Constitution. He was the chief recorder of the convention, and it is through his writings that we have learned so much of what went on during our country's early years. James also coauthored the Federalist Papers, with Alexander Hamilton and John Jay.

James Madison was always interested in preserving the freedom of religion, and he drafted Virginia's law that protected the right to worship any religion. Later, as a U.S. congressman, he sponsored the first ten amendments to the Constitution, which are known as the Bill of Rights. These amendments guarantee many rights, including the freedoms of speech, the press, and religion.

In 1794, James married Dolley Payne Todd, a beautiful young Quaker widow. Her husband and baby had died during an epidemic of yellow fever in

Philadelphia. Dolley Madison was a lively woman who brought much happiness to James' life. She became known for the fancy clothes she wore and for her fabulous parties.

James Madison became the secretary of state for President Thomas Jefferson in 1801. And eight years later, James Madison was elected president of the United States. He served for two terms as president, and led the country through the War of 1812.

England and France had been at war, and the people of the United States were divided over whom to support. France had helped the United States during the Revolutionary War, but most Americans were of English ancestry. James Madison wanted to stay neutral in the war, even though he still resented England because of the Revolutionary War. But England ruled the seas, and the British Navy terrorized American ships. The English sailors would board American ships by force, looking for English deserters. Then, they would capture many sailors, most of whom were Americans. James demanded that the English ships stop, but they ignored him. So, the United States was forced, once again, to go to war with England.

The war started out badly, with the Americans losing battles. But James Madison replaced many of his generals, and the newer, younger generals began winning great victories. At one point, the English landed near Washington and began a march on the city. The American government, including James and Dolley Madison, escaped to Virginia. As the English soldiers advanced on the city, Dolley Madison rescued many important papers from the White House, including the original Declaration of Independence and George Washington's papers. The English moved in and burned almost all the government buildings in Washington, including the White House.

After the English soldiers left Washington, the Madisons returned and lived with relatives while the White House was being repaired. President Madison put Gen. Andrew Jackson in charge of the American troops defending New Orleans, which was the most important port for the entire Mississippi River valley. His forces defeated a larger English Army, and the Americans suffered only small losses. But the soldiers on both sides did not know that by the time of the battle, the English had already agreed to a peace treaty with America.

When the war ended, James Madison was a hero to the American people. He convinced the Congress to keep a standing army, and to raise taxes to pay for it. The United States was on its way to becoming a world power.

When James Madison left the presidency, he retired to his estate at Montpelier, and managed the 5,000 acres of farmland. He kept up his long friendship with Thomas Jefferson, who had already retired to Monticello. And James had collected a library of over 4,000 books, as he could read in seven languages. He spent his time editing his papers, and advising the U.S. and Virginia governments.

James Madison left his mark on the American nation, fighting for the basic rights and freedoms of its people, and defending it against foreign aggression.

GEORGE MASON
(1725-1792)

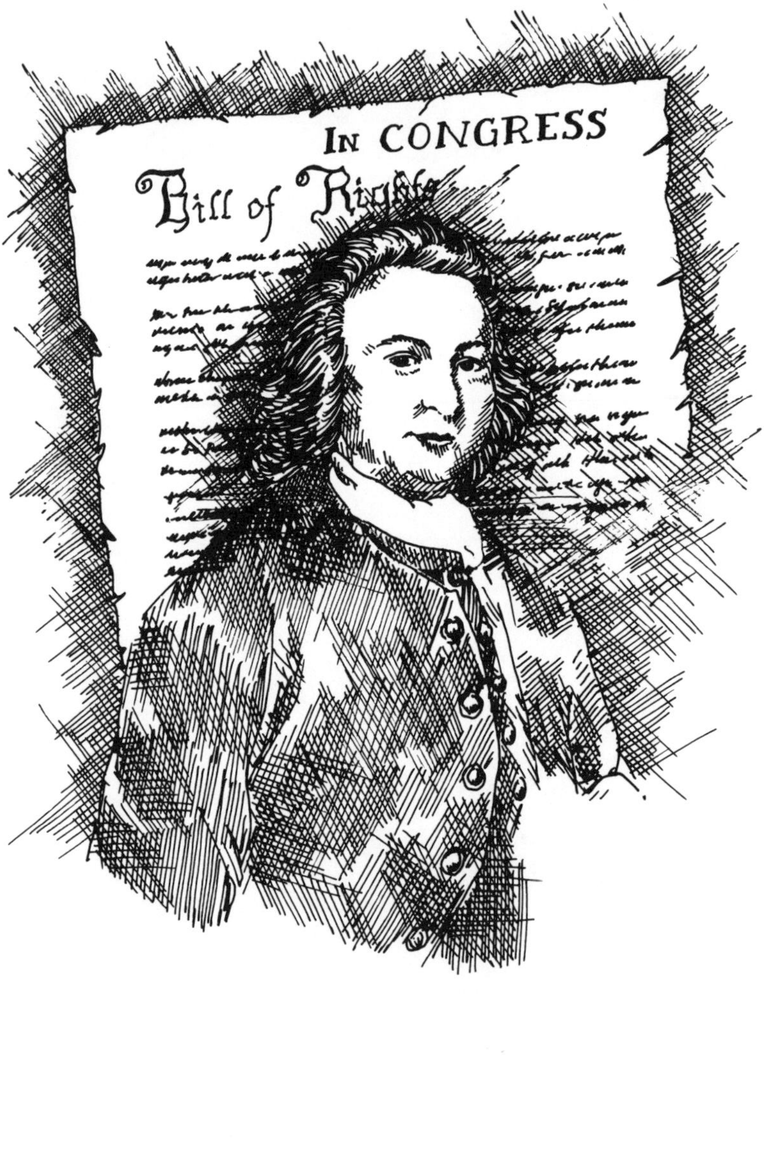
In CONGRESS
Bill of Rights

. . . the reluctant patriot

TODAY WHEN WE THINK of the great founding fathers of the United States, we usually think of such men as Washington, Jefferson, Adams, and Franklin. Not many people give George Mason the credit he deserves, although in his lifetime his name was often mentioned with those other great Americans. Toward the end of his life, George Mason disagreed with the majority who signed the U.S. Constitution. When he died, some people thought he had turned his back on the country he had helped to create. But nothing could have been farther from the truth.

George Mason was born in Fairfax County, the oldest of three children. His father was a wealthy English planter who owned land in Virginia and Maryland. A terrible tragedy happened when George was nine. His father drowned while crossing the Potomac River from Maryland to Virginia.

Fortunately, there were many family members and friends for the young Mason children. After receiving tutoring as a youth, George went to study with his uncle, John Mercer, who was a lawyer. John Mercer had one of the largest libraries in Virginia, and George read and studied the classics, the law, and ideas of famous philosophers. George read books that talked about the natural rights to which all men were entitled, and he read about the evils of slavery. These were lessons that George Mason would remember for the rest of his life.

When George turned twenty-one, he received his inheritance of thousands of acres of farmland in Virginia and Maryland. At the age of twenty-five, he married Ann Eilbeck, who was a sixteen-year-old beauty. They settled in Fairfax County at Gunston Hall, a home that George had built for his family. The Masons eventually had nine children, all of whom survived childhood. It was a very rare thing to have all of one's children survive in George Mason's day, because of childhood diseases for which there were no cures.

George was very active in the development of the Virginia colony. He served as justice of the peace in Fairfax County, and he would often ride into Alexandria with his good friend and neighbor George Washington. George Mason and George Washington visited each other often, and they exchanged seeds and tree grafts from their estates.

Although George Mason was elected to the House of Burgesses in 1759, he did not seem to be interested in a life of politics. He suffered from poor health for most of his life, and he did not like to travel far from home. He passed up opportunities to serve when it would have meant time away from his family.

But George was interested in expanding the colonies. He was active in the Ohio Company, which sold land on the upper Ohio River. He also bought land to expand his own holdings. In his time, the oldest son in the family usually inherited all the family's land. But George made sure that all of his children would be provided for after his death.

Ann Eilbeck Mason died in 1773, when she was only thirty-nine. George never recovered from his wife's death, and he felt an even greater need to stay at Gunston Hall with his children. But in 1776, he was asked to take George Washington's place at the Virginia Constitutional Convention. He wrote the Virginia constitution, and much of what he wrote inspired Thomas Jefferson, when he wrote the Declaration of Independence.

George Mason served in the Virginia House of Delegates from 1776 to 1788. He was a member of the Virginia delegation to the U.S. Constitutional Convention. Like many other Virginians, George was worried that the new constitution being drafted would not protect the rights of the people. He also opposed a compromise that allowed Southern states to import slaves for another twenty years. He wanted slavery to come to an end, but other states' delegations would never agree to that.

In the end, George refused to sign the new U.S. Constitution. But because of his strong views on personal freedom, others were inspired to work for a Bill of Rights, which became the first ten amendments to the U.S. Constitution.

George Mason retired to Gunston Hall, and because of his views opposing the Constitution, he was abandoned by many people. But gradually, people began to realize that his opinions were correct in many ways. Even though he was older than most of the other founding fathers, his ideas showed him to be ahead of his time. He supported civil liberties and an end to slavery, and most of his ideas have become law in the years since his death.

CYRUS McCORMICK
(1809-1884)

. . . reaper man

AMERICA IN THE 1800s was an expanding nation. With each passing year, more settlers moved westward, in search of a better life. For some, the search was for furs or gold. For others, the search was for large parcels of fertile farmland. There were many hazards for these settlers, such as wild animals, hostile Indians, extremes of climate, and uncharted rivers and mountain ranges.

Food was needed to feed the growing number of settlers, and farm labor was in short supply. Fortunately, the efforts of a young Virginian to mechanize the harvest had begun to pay off. Cyrus McCormick and his mechanical reaper are credited with helping to push back the western frontier of the United States by fifty miles every year.

For a while, it looked as though Cyrus's father would be able to make the first working mechanical reaper. Robert McCormick was a farmer, a blacksmith, and an inventor. He had already invented a threshing machine and a self-sharpening plow. But he had failed in his many attempts to make a mechanical reaper. He recognized that a mechanical reaper would be of great benefit to farmers everywhere. When a crop ripened, it was important to harvest it right away. And reaping was hard, backbreaking work that required many slaves or fieldworkers.

The McCormick family lived in Rockbridge County on Walnut Grove Farm. Cyrus's great-grandparents were of Scotch descent, but they came to America from Ireland. Cyrus was the eldest son in the family, so he worked closely with his father on the farm. When the family built a new house, they built it using only materials that came from the farm. They made their own bricks, and they made all the nails and other hardware in their blacksmith shop.

Cyrus's father worked very hard to build a mechanical reaper. He knew that he would be able to plant a much larger crop only if there was a way that he could harvest it before it spoiled. In 1816, he tested his reaper but found that it would not cut wet grain. He forgot about his invention for a while, but Cyrus decided to try his own hand at it.

First, he made a different kind of design, and he made several small models to see if they would work. When he was satisfied with his design, he built a full-scale horse-drawn model.

In 1831, Cyrus put his reaper to the test. The first reapers were so noisy that slaves had to walk alongside the horses to keep them calm. But the reaper worked, and soon the McCormick Virginia Reaper was doing the work of five men. Cyrus was only twenty-two years old at the time!

Cyrus and his father started an iron ore smelting plant that they called the Cotopaxi Iron Works, named for a mountain in South America. But hard economic times forced them out of business.

Cyrus started to sell his reapers, one at a time, to people from Virginia. But soon, Cyrus realized that there was a greater need for his reapers in the midwestern part of the United States. It was hard for Cyrus to transport his reapers across the Appalachian Mountains. So he moved to Chicago and opened a factory from which he could sell his reapers. Chicago was a center for transportation with easy access to the newly opening farmlands of the Midwest.

Cyrus McCormick was a shrewd businessman. He knew that some farmers did not believe that a mechanical reaper would work. So, he offered a warranty on his reapers, and he allowed farmers to pay for their reapers over a period of time.

The McCormick reaper factory prospered, and Cyrus McCormick's fame spread across the Atlantic Ocean. One of his reapers was on display at the American pavilion at the London World's Fair in 1851, where it won the Grand Prize. The reaper also won the Grand Medal of Honor at the International Exposition in Paris in 1855. In 1861, over 6,000 reapers were sold.

Cyrus McCormick never forgot his native Virginia. After the Civil War ended in 1865, he sent large gifts of money to schools and seminaries in Virginia and other Southern states.

In 1871, the great Chicago fire destroyed Cyrus McCormick's factory. Many people expected that Cyrus would simply retire, since he had already made his fortune. But he rebuilt his factory, and it grew to be bigger than ever.

The company became known as the International Harvester Company when it merged with other companies that made farm machinery. Cyrus McCormick's son, Cyrus, Jr., and his grandson continued in the family's business for many years after Cyrus's death in 1884.

JAMES MONROE
(1758-1831)

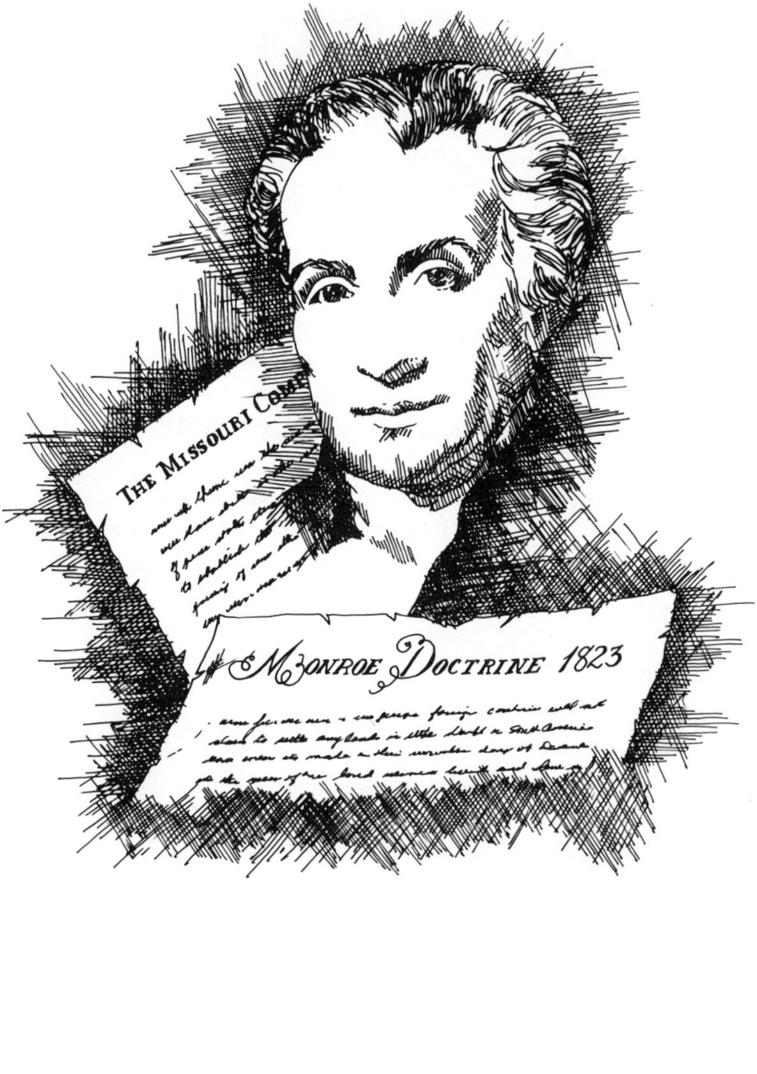

THE MISSOURI COMP
MONROE DOCTRINE 1823

... *"The Era of Good Feeling"*

GEORGE WASHINGTON and James Monroe were the only two veterans of the American Revolutionary War who went on to become presidents of the United States. Both men were from Virginia, and as presidents, both men were very concerned with America's relations with other countries.

James Monroe was one of the most enthusiastic supporters of the American cause, and at an early age. He was born in Westmoreland County, Virginia, to Spence Monroe, who was Scottish, and Eliza Jones Monroe, who was Welsh. Spence Monroe was a tobacco farmer, but he was also a carpenter and a cabinetmaker.

James' early life was fairly typical for a boy of his time. He learned to hunt and fish at an early age. When he was eleven years old, he was able to attend a private academy where he learned Latin and mathematics. Most young men in James' time did not receive any formal education.

When James was fifteen years old, his father died. But by that time, James' father and uncle had already decided that he should study law. He went to the College of William and Mary in Williamsburg, at about the same time that unrest was beginning to grow in the colonies.

On James' seventeenth birthday, he left William and Mary to join the militia in the fight against the British. James and other students broke into the palace of the governor and took muskets. He joined the Third Virginia Regiment and later fought in Revolutionary War battles at White Plains, Brandywine, Monmouth, and

Trenton. James crossed the icy Delaware River with Gen. George Washington to fight in the battle of Trenton, where he was seriously wounded in the shoulder. He rejoined his regiment the following summer and was promoted to major. Later, he was promoted to colonel in the Virginia regiment.

After the end of the Revolutionary War, James Monroe studied law in Virginia with Thomas Jefferson. They became friends and remained friends for the rest of their lives.

Because of James' war record and the high praise he received from George Washington, he was elected to the Virginia House of Delegates and Congress. He soon married Elizabeth Kortright, who came from a well-to-do family in New York.

Like some other Virginians, James Monroe voted against the U.S. Constitution because it did not include a bill of rights for its individual citizens. But a bill of rights was later added to the Constitution. James served as a U.S. senator from 1790 to 1794. From that point, he began to hold a long series of important government offices.

He served as a minister to France while George Washington was president, and again in 1803. He took part in the negotiations that led to the Louisiana Purchase. He also served as governor of Virginia from 1799 to 1802, then again in 1811. He served as a minister to Great Britain, then ran unsuccessfully for president against James Madison. He later served as secretary of state in President Madison's cabinet from 1811 to 1817.

James Monroe's years as secretary of state were difficult ones. The United States was involved in the War of 1812 against Great Britain. For a while, the war went very badly for the Americans. The British invaded Washington, D.C. and burned most of the government buildings. Afterwards, James was also given the jobs of secretary of war and military commander for the District of Columbia.

In 1816, James Monroe was elected to be the fifth president of the United States. Of the first five presidents, four—Washington, Jefferson, Madison, and Monroe—were from Virginia. After he was inaugurated, James Monroe took a three-month tour of the country, to talk to people in different regions. He wanted to heal the wounds of the nation that remained after the War of 1812.

James Monroe was a very popular president. He governed the United States during a period of great expansion and prosperity. His years as president were known as "The Era of Good Feeling," because people felt so good about themselves and their country. James Monroe ran unopposed for reelection in 1820.

The issue of slavery was becoming very important during James Monroe's presidency. As new states were added to the Union, the Northern states wanted to prohibit slavery, while the Southern states wanted slavery to continue. James signed the Missouri Compromise, which allowed Missouri to enter the Union as a slave state, but only if Maine was allowed to enter the Union as a free state.

James Monroe also supported a plan that would have gradually freed the slaves in the South and returned them to Africa. Land was bought in Africa, and the country of Liberia was created. The capital city, Monrovia, was named for James Monroe. But many of the blacks who went to Africa found it difficult to live in Liberia, since few of them had been born in Africa. Most had been born and raised on plantations in America.

In 1823, James Monroe issued a policy that came to be known as the Monroe Doctrine. It stated that the

United States would not interfere in European wars, and that European countries did not have the right to colonize any more land in North or South America. It was a bold policy that James made. The United States had already defeated Great Britain twice, and America was willing to fight in order to protect its interests.

When James Monroe's second term as president was over in 1825, the Monroes left Washington and retired to their home at Oak Hill, near Leesburg. Thomas Jefferson had designed the house for the Monroes, and it had an oak tree on its lawn for each of the states in the Union. But the Monroes' retirement was not happy. Because of bad financial problems, James was forced to sell his land in Kentucky and Virginia. Then, Elizabeth died in 1830. James sold Oak Hill and moved to New York City, to live with his daughter and her husband. Less than a year later, he died—on July 4, 1831. He was the third president who died on the Fourth of July.

The Monroe Doctrine became the cornerstone of American foreign policy for many years. European countries no longer colonized the Western Hemisphere, and the United States did not fight in a European war until World War I. But by then, the United States had grown even larger and stronger and was ready to take its place as a world power.

POCAHONTAS
(1595-1617)

... Indian princess and English lady

THE INDIAN PRINCESS POCAHONTAS is most famous for the story of how, as a young girl, she rescued Capt. John Smith from being killed by the Indians. According to Captain Smith, he was captured by the Indians and sentenced to death. Pocahontas intervened and begged her father to spare Smith's life, and he was set free. This story may be only a legend. But the true story of Pocahontas's life is more interesting and remarkable than any legend could ever be.

In 1607, English settlers arrived in Virginia and built a settlement known as Jamestown at the mouth of the James River. In a short time, they learned that they had landed in the heart of the Chickahominy Indian nation. The Indian lands extended roughly from present-day Pennsylvania to North Carolina. In fact, the chief of the Chickahominy, Powhatan, lived only a short two or three days' journey from Jamestown.

Chief Powhatan had a daughter, Pocahontas, who was only twelve years old when the English arrived. Pocahontas's mother had died while giving birth, so Pocahontas was raised by her aunts.

Pocahontas was a tomboy and was able to run, hunt, shoot arrows, and throw an ax as well as many boys her age.

At first, the Indians did not think that the small English settlement of 152 men was a threat to them. Relations were good between the English and the Indians, and the Indians helped the English survive. In fact, each winter the English settlers needed to trade some of their iron cookware and blankets for food and furs. Although the English had guns, which the Indians called "fire-sticks," they were not very accurate and could not be used very successfully for hunting.

In 1610, when Pocahontas was fifteen, she travelled for the first time to the Jamestown settlement with her father and brothers. By this time, more settlers had arrived, including the new governor, Lord de la Warr.

Pocahontas was very curious about the English and their way of life. The English were also very curious about her, and they invited her into their homes. She so charmed the English ladies that they presented her with an outfit of English clothing, which she wore when she returned to Jamestown the next year.

Shortly later, relations between the English and the Chickahominy began to worsen. The Indians realized that the English now had enough men and weapons to defeat them if a war were to break out. Since the English still needed to trade with the Indians for some of their food, the Indians demanded a large amount of guns and ammunition. The Indians threatened to stop trading altogether unless they received the weapons. The English refused to trade their weapons, and they began to fear an attack by the Indians.

One of the colonists hatched a secret plot to keep the Indians from attacking. He travelled to the Indian village and pretended that the colonists had decided to trade guns to the Indians. Once he was there, he took the opportunity to kidnap Pocahontas and take her with him to Jamestown.

When a Chickahominy woman was captured by an enemy, she was no longer considered to be a part of the tribe. Pocahontas stayed in Jamestown and lived in the house of the deputy governor and his wife, Sir Thomas Dale and Lady Dale. Pocahontas learned English by reading the new King James Version Bible and took on English habits. But she also introduced many new wild foods into the colonists' diets and taught them how to roast meats.

In 1613, Pocahontas was baptized into the Anglican church. This created a great sensation in Virginia and in England, as she was the first Indian converted to Christianity.

The following year, when she was nineteen, Pocahontas met and married John Rolfe. Rolfe had been part of an expedition to Jamestown in 1610 that was forced by a storm to land in Bermuda. John Rolfe was a widower with two children, Barbara and John, from his first marriage. He had come to the New World to seek his fortune as a tobacco farmer.

In 1615, Pocahontas and John Rolfe had a son of their own, whom they named Thomas. Pocahontas often took her child and her stepchildren on visits to her Indian family in the Chickahominy village.

Back in England, King James continued to send prisoners to Jamestown as their punishment. But many of these people were not suited to life in the colony and many had no job skills to offer. The leaders of the Jamestown colony decided that something had to be done to attract new settlers. They decided that John Rolfe, Pocahontas, and their children should visit England to encourage more people to come to Virginia. John and Pocahontas were willing to go. John needed to raise money to expand his tobacco farming. Tobacco had become very popular in England, and he thought his business could be very profitable.

The people in London heard about plans for the Rolfes' trip. When their ship arrived, hundreds of people were waiting at the dock to catch a glimpse of the Indian princess who was now a proper English lady. Pocahontas was friendly and happy to meet people, and she attracted a following wherever she went.

Pocahontas and John Rolfe attended many parties

and receptions that were held in their honor. Finally, Queen Anne invited Pocahontas to a visit at the royal residence. The queen and her son, Prince Charles, were delighted by Pocahontas and invited her to return many times. Later, Pocahontas met King James, who was impressed with her ability to quote many long passages from the Bible.

The Rolfes' visit to England was a great success. John Rolfe was able to obtain the money he needed for his tobacco business. Pocahontas's many public appearances prompted many working people and tradesmen to move to Jamestown.

By the fall of 1617, the Rolfes were eager to return to Virginia. John Rolfe wanted to return to farming, while Pocahontas wanted to visit with her Indian family.

Pocahontas fainted at one of the many banquets that were given before the Rolfes departed. When their ship finally left London on November 5, she seemed weak and decided to rest in the ship's cabin. The following day, while their ship was passing through the English Channel, Pocahontas died. She was twenty-two years old.

Pocahontas was buried in England. The exact cause of her death was never discovered. The queen, prince, and many other important people attended her funeral service. John Rolfe eventually returned to Virginia, where he became a successful planter. He finally returned to England to live with his oldest child. But Thomas, Pocahontas's son, returned to Virginia and became the colony's wealthiest tobacco planter.

Many prominent Virginians since colonial days have proudly claimed Pocahontas and Thomas Rolfe as their ancestors.

CHIEF POWHATAN
(1548?-1618)

...Indian chief

VERY LITTLE IS KNOWN about the life of Powhatan before 1607, when the English settlers arrived at Jamestown. He was born Wahunsacock, but he took the name of Powhatan when he succeeded his father as chief of the Powhatan confederacy.

Powhatan's father was a chief of the Algonquian Indian nation, and he moved south to Virginia in the 1500s. He conquered five other tribes and set up a confederacy. After Powhatan succeeded his father, he conquered about two dozen other neighboring tribes, each of which had its own chief. It is believed that Powhatan ruled over about 9,000 Indians, who lived in about 160 villages in what is now eastern Virginia.

Powhatan's capital was located in the village of Werowocomoco, on the north bank of the York River. Powhatan, as chief, had over 100 wives and many children, including the famous princess Pocahontas.

When the English settlers arrived, they found the Indians living a primitive existence. But the settlers soon learned that the Indians were skilled at feeding and caring for themselves. The Indians hunted deer and bear, fished, gathered fruit, and grew maize and peas.

The Powhatan Indians worshipped the sun as a god. They believed in the god Ahone, who governed the world and was responsible for everything that was good. They also believed in the god Okee, who caused all the evil in the world.

The English settlers came to the New World in search of gold, in the same way that the Spanish had earlier found gold in Mexico and Peru. But they told the Indians that they had been blown off course from their planned destination. Soon, the settlers began building a fort and houses. The Indians quickly realized that the English planned to stay.

Powhatan was described by Capt. John Smith, one of the colonists, as being about sixty years old when they met in 1608. Captain Smith wrote that Powhatan was tall, in good physical condition, and had a thin beard.

It was soon clear to the Indians that the colonists did not know how to hunt or grow native food. If Powhatan had not sent food to the settlers on a number of occasions, they surely would have starved. When a fire broke out in Jamestown in the first year and burned down all but three small buildings, Powhatan sent food to help the colonists.

Capt. John Smith learned the Indian language and gained Powhatan's respect. Captain Smith was befriended by Pocahontas, and Powhatan "adopted" Captain Smith and gave him the Indian name "Nantaquod."

Still, the Indians and the colonists fought often, because the colonists wanted more land to grow food and expand their settlement. The colonists began trading with the Indians for food. They gave the Indians beads and cookware, but the Indians wanted some of the colonists' guns and cannons. The colonists wisely refused to trade their weapons. But the Indians still managed to capture some guns during some of the raids they would make on the colonists.

Some of the colonists worked out a plan to kidnap Pocahontas, in the hope that having her as a hostage would protect them from further Indian attacks. Once they kidnapped her, they offered her safe return in exchange for all the weapons that the Indians had captured and all their English prisoners. Indians did not usually pay ransom when one of their women was taken hostage. But finally, after three months, Powhatan offered to exchange seven broken muskets, seven English captives, and a promise of 500 bushels of corn. He said that the rest of the captured weapons had been lost or stolen.

But Pocahontas had a surprise for her father. While living at Jamestown, she converted to Christianity, and met and fell in love with one of the colonists, John Rolfe. When Powhatan heard of his daughter's plans to marry, he knew there was no need to turn over his weapons. Pocahontas was no longer a hostage to the English.

Powhatan did not attend his daughter's wedding, but he gave some gifts to the new couple. He gave them a tract of land on the James River, and he presented a freshwater-pearl necklace to Pocahontas that she wore at her wedding.

The Jamestown settlers thought there would at last be peace with the Indians. They wanted to give a crown to Powhatan, and they wanted him to pledge his loyalty to King James in England. They also brought Powhatan gifts of a new bed, rings, and a scarlet coat. But Powhatan refused to kneel to be crowned. He considered himself to be an equal to the English king.

A period of peace did begin, but it was not to last. Powhatan moved to a village farther away from Jamestown. Powhatan's brother, Opechancanough, wanted to wipe out the English. His followers began to starve out the colonists, and they killed as many colonists as they could whenever the settlers ventured out of the fort.

But the colonists learned that the Indians' tobacco was a valuable crop that could be sold in England. The colonists had already begun to smoke tobacco, and many Europeans also wanted to smoke it. More colonists arrived to plant tobacco, and they were determined to stay. Even though the fighting continued between the colonists and the Indians, the colonists kept up their demands for more land.

After Powhatan died in 1618, his brother, Opechancanough, became chief. He continued to attack the colonists whenever he could. The last Indian uprising took place in 1644, but Opechancanough was killed. The Indians were no match for the colonists' supply of guns and cannons.

By 1700, the Indians that had survived were scattered and could not organize any resistance to the growing English presence. There are now about 3,000 descendents of the Powhatan Indians in Virginia, most of whom live in the eastern part of the state.

SIR WALTER RALEIGH
(1552?-1618)

. . . lord and governor of Virginia

SIR WALTER RALEIGH was one of the most colorful and influential men of the Elizabethan Age in England. But his life was also one of the most tragic. He was a close friend and adviser to Queen Elizabeth I, but he lost favor several times at court and was eventually beheaded by order of King James I.

Sir Walter Raleigh was one of those rare men who succeeded at many things. He was an explorer, a soldier, a sailor, a poet, and a scientist. And he was responsible, perhaps more than any other person, for England's exploration and settling of Virginia. For without his efforts to start an English settlement in Virginia, the land might well have been settled by the Spanish, who had already explored Central and South America.

Walter Raleigh was born around 1552 in Devonshire, England. He came from a respectable English family, but his father did not own the land that he farmed. Walter was determined to become wealthy and successful, and he decided that the best way to do this was by becoming a soldier. He left Oxford University, without graduating, to fight in the French Civil War. In several years he came back to England as an experienced soldier. He fought in Ireland against rebel forces and very bravely defended his men against a much larger force.

When he returned to England he was taken to the royal court, where he met Queen Elizabeth I. He impressed her with his ideas about the Irish rebellion. She took the time to learn more about this dashing young man, who was intelligent and had a sharp wit.

Once, when walking with the queen, Walter Raleigh laid down his finest cloak on the ground to keep the queen from stepping into a puddle. The queen was charmed by his action and rewarded him by buying him many expensive suits of clothing.

The queen also gave Walter Raleigh the use of land and a manor house, and gave him control over the exportation of wine and broadcloth. Almost overnight, Walter was a wealthy man. He was knighted in 1585 and he became captain of the queen's guard two years later.

But Sir Walter Raleigh had his eye on even greater fortune. The Spanish explorers of the time had already discovered Mexico and Peru and brought back shiploads of gold and precious jewels to their country. Raleigh and other Englishmen hoped to do the same for their queen. He thought that he could find a passage to the Orient, as well as gold and other riches.

Walter used his new fortune to help finance the discovery of the New World. The queen named him lord and governor of Virginia. On one of the expeditions that Walter organized, one of his half-brothers, Sir Humphrey Gilbert, was lost at sea in a violent storm. And although he organized several other expeditions, including the famous Lost Colony, he was never allowed to travel with the expedition. The queen wanted Walter to stay with her at court.

Walter lost favor with the queen when she found out about his secret marriage to one of her maids of honor. Walter wanted to get back into the queen's favor, so he organized an expedition to South America. He went looking for the fabled gold city of El Dorado. When he left South America, he tried to travel north to visit the Virginia colony, but bad weather kept him away, and forced him to return to England.

Queen Elizabeth I died in 1603, and she was succeeded by the Scottish king James I. King James was told that Sir Walter Raleigh opposed him, so the king had Walter put into prison, charging him with treason. Walter spent thirteen years in prison, where he wrote a history of the world for the king's son, Prince Henry, and did scientific experiments with plants that had been brought back from the New World.

When Sir Walter Raleigh was finally released from prison, it was to go searching once again for gold in South America. Before his trip, he had been warned against fighting the Spanish troops there. Once in South America, Walter and his men treated the native Indians with respect, unlike the Spanish colonists who had brutalized the Indians. But while Walter and his men were in South America, fighting broke out with the Spanish. Walter's son was killed, as were many Spanish soldiers.

Sir Walter Raleigh returned to England, knowing that he would face prison once again, and maybe execution. Even though Walter had acted in self-defense, the Spanish king persuaded King James to execute Walter for his part in the death of the Spanish soldiers in South America.

Sir Walter Raleigh died as a hero to his fellow Englishmen. He was responsible for England's continued efforts to colonize the New World. And although he never was able to visit Virginia, he was largely responsible for the colony's eventual success.

WALTER REED
(1851-1902)

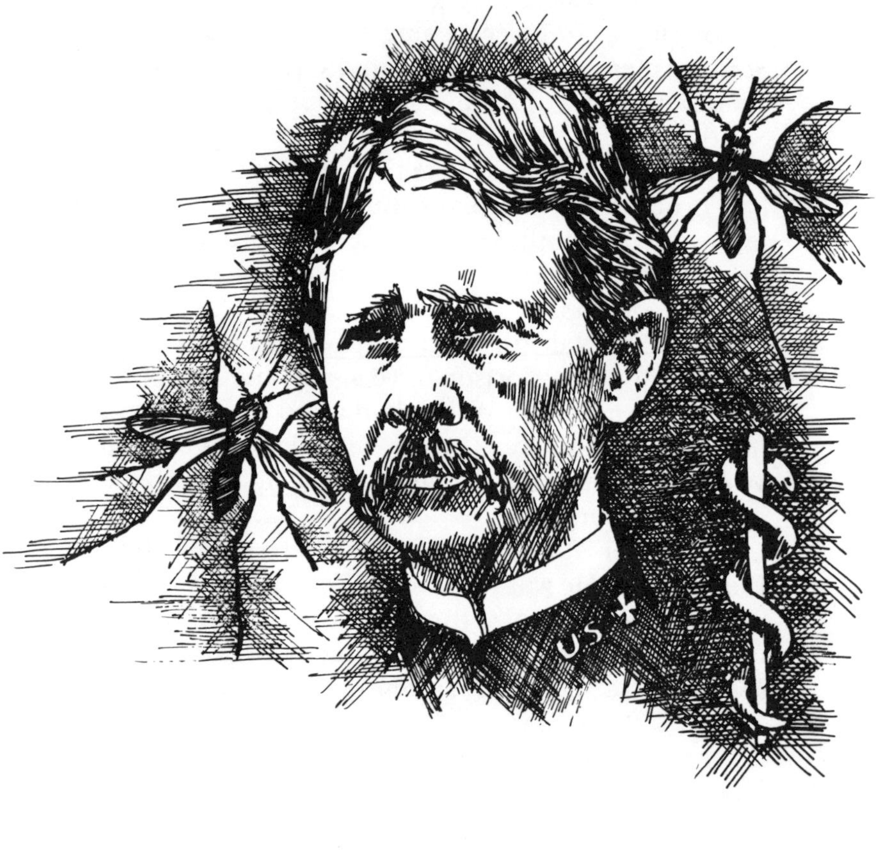
US

... conqueror of yellow fever

THE LATE 1800s were a difficult time to be an Army doctor. Pay was low, and the conditions that doctors endured were terrible. Many of the Army posts were in desolate, distant places where there were great dangers of disease and Indian attacks. It was under these kinds of conditions that Walter Reed was able to make his great contributions to the world of medicine.

Walter's father was a Methodist minister, and the Reed family moved several times from Walter's birthplace in Gloucester County, Virginia. Walter Reed was the youngest of five children, and he grew up during the Civil War. His two oldest brothers fought in the war, and one of them lost an arm.

Toward the end of the war, when he was thirteen, Walter and his brother were given the job of hiding the family's horses from the approaching Union army soldiers. They were discovered by the soldiers and had to give up the horses, and Walter felt that he had disappointed his father. But his father was glad that his sons were unhurt.

Even after the war ended, the Reed family suffered hardships. Walter's mother had been sick with asthma, and she died when Walter was fourteen. He passed her grave every day while walking to school, and perhaps her death inspired him to become a doctor so he could help people who were sick.

Walter's father asked the Methodist church for an assignment near Charlottesville so his children could go to the University of Virginia. So, after attending private schools in the area, Walter entered the University of Virginia and earned a medical degree in only two years. He was the youngest person to graduate from there with a medical degree.

Still, Walter knew that he needed more education. So he enrolled at the Bellevue Hospital Medical College in New York and earned a second medical degree in 1870. He worked for a while for the Board of Health for New York and Brooklyn. But Walter wanted adventure, so he applied for a position with the U.S. Army. He was commissioned as an assistant surgeon in the Army and a first lieutenant in 1875.

As a young Army doctor, Walter Reed was assigned to many frontier posts in Indian territory. Just before he left for Fort Yuma in California, he married Emilie Lawrence. She joined him out West, and they spent eleven years at assignments in California, Arizona, Nebraska, and Alabama. They had a daughter, and they adopted an Indian girl who had been injured.

Time passed, and Walter Reed realized that the world of medicine was changing. Microscopes were becoming widely used in discovering the causes of illnesses. Walter was able to study at Johns Hopkins Hospital in Baltimore, and he became a professor of bacteriology at the Army Medical School in Washington. From 1893 to 1900, he performed experiments on communicable diseases such as typhoid fever and yellow fever. During the Spanish-American War, he investigated an epidemic of typhoid fever among American troops, and helped to prevent other outbreaks. He had sick soldiers quarantined, and he had the area around the camp cleaned up to prevent other cases of the disease.

But another killer disease had to be fought. Yellow fever was spreading among the U.S. soldiers in Cuba. In fact, more soldiers died from yellow fever than from bullets during the Spanish-American War. And every year, yellow fever killed hundreds of people in the United States, mostly in warm climates during the hotter months.

Yellow fever was a terrible disease. It was not usually fatal, but its victims could die horrible, painful deaths. Walter Reed was appointed to head a commission to investigate the cause and method of transmission of yellow fever.

A local doctor in Cuba had a theory that yellow fever might be spread by a certain species of mosquitoes, but he didn't know how to test his theory. Almost everyone else thought the disease was spread through infected clothing and linens.

Walter Reed and the other doctors could never find a germ or bacteria that caused yellow fever. But they were able to prove how yellow fever was spread. Since animals did not catch yellow fever, Reed used human volunteers to test his theory. There was no other way to prove how the disease was spread. Most of the volunteers got sick, and a few died. But the scientists could prove, once and for all, how the disease was spread.

The doctors learned that a mosquito that bit an infected person could infect other people. But this could only happen after the disease had a chance to develop in the mosquito's body. There was no cure for yellow fever, but there was a way to end the outbreak of the disease. They had to rid the island of the disease-carrying mosquitoes.

By killing the mosquitoes, yellow fever was wiped out in Cuba in three months. In 1900, there were 1,400 cases of yellow fever in Havana, Cuba. But by 1902, there were no cases at all.

Walter Reed returned to Washington and resumed teaching at the Army Medical School. He received honorary degrees from Harvard University and the University of Michigan. But he was not able to enjoy his fame for long. In 1902, he died suddenly of a ruptured appendix. His work has earned him a place among the giants in the history of medicine. The Walter Reed Army Medical Center in Washington was named in his honor.

BILL ("BOJANGLES") ROBINSON
(1878-1949)

... "Mr. Bojangles"

IT IS NO EXAGGERATION to state that Bill Robinson was the best-loved and most widely known black American entertainer of his day. His dancing career included decades of performances in vaudeville, in the theater, and in movies. Yet most people today only know him because of his nickname, "Mr. Bojangles."

Bill Robinson grew up in Richmond in the 1880s, dancing for pennies on street corners. Many of the facts about his early years are a mystery to us. No one is certain whether he was really born in 1878. His parents, Maxwell and Maria Robinson, were both dead by 1885, but no one is sure how they died. There are stories about how Bill acquired the nickname "Mr. Bojangles" and how he met the man who encouraged his career. But one thing is not a mystery: Bill Robinson was the greatest American dancer of the early twentieth century.

"Bojangles" was a tap dancer. But, like many black American performers of his day, his opportunities were limited. Normally, black entertainers were not allowed to perform for white audiences except in minor roles. So, Bill spent a lot of time as a youth dancing in front of theaters in Richmond, hoping to get pennies from people who were entering the theater.

Bill's grandmother raised him after his parents died, but she did not encourage his dancing. She had been a slave and she was a very strict Baptist woman. She believed that dancing was evil, and she would not allow Bill to dance or even talk about dancing in her home.

When he was twelve years old, Bill and a friend hopped onto a train and left Richmond for Washington, D.C.

Bill took a job rubbing down horses after their races and workouts, but he continued to dance whenever he got the chance. He had a small part in an all-black musical comedy called *The South Before the War*. His big break came when he met Marty Forkins, who was to be Bill's manager for the rest of his life. Bill told a story about how they met. Bill was working as a waiter, and he accidently dumped a bowl of oyster stew on Marty's lap. Bill then apologized and told him that he really wasn't a waiter, but that he was really a dancer. After agreeing to see Bill perform, Marty decided to be his manager.

Bill Robinson gained a lot of experience by working in minstrel shows. They were live performances that gave an idealized view of the lives of slaves on a plantation. Minstrel shows usually included jokes, dances, and songs, and Bill was able to tour across the country with several shows. Bill also worked with dance partners in performances, but he was always the more talented dancer. He travelled to New York, Denver, and Boston, and even made it to London, where he was a big hit.

He created many new dance steps, but he was most famous for his stair dance. It was so popular that he made it a part of every performance. He had a set of portable stairs made that he would take with him from theater to theater. Many people copied Bill's stair dance, and Bill tried (unsuccessfully) to have his dance patented.

People were taking notice of Bojangles. He took every opportunity to perform wherever he could, and he was a total professional in his work. He performed in all-black revues, plays, and movies, and he was finally able to get parts in some Hollywood productions. He could not always fight against prejudice, because he knew that it was important for people to enjoy working with him. He was able to integrate the world of white entertainment, which in turn opened the doors for other black performers.

Bojangles was a tireless performer, and he sometimes danced as many as twelve performances in a single day. He danced so much that he wore out between twenty and thirty pairs of shoes every year!

Bill Robinson was also famous for his unusual ability to run backwards. No one is sure how he learned to do it, but he could run backwards faster than most people could run forward. For many years, he held the world's record for running backwards. He once ran seventy-five yards backwards in a little more than eight seconds!

Later in his life, Bill Robinson starred in several movies with the famous child star Shirley Temple. He taught her the stair dance, which they danced together in the movies. They remained friends for the rest of his life. In all, Bill Robinson appeared in fourteen movies, and at the height of his career he was earning $6,600 per week.

Still, Bill Robinson was never wealthy. He lost much of his money gambling, and he was always generous to others. He gave money to people who needed help, and he sent money home to Richmond for schools and orphanages. He spent much of his time performing to raise money for a number of charities.

About a year before he died, he suffered a heart attack and had cataract surgery on his eyes. But as soon as he was well, he resumed dancing until he could no longer see the stairs in his stair dance routines.

Over 10,000 cards and letters were sent to the hospital in the last week of Bill Robinson's life. Get-well wishes arrived from President Truman and from other famous persons. When he died, his funeral in New York was the largest in the city's history. Over

50,000 people lined the streets for the funeral procession. A large banner was hung from a theater that read, "SO LONG, BILL ROBINSON. HIS FEET BROUGHT JOY TO THE WORLD."

Many people have wondered where the nickname "Bojangles" came from. Some of Bill's childhood friends had stories that they thought explained the name's origin. The word "bojangles" refers to someone who is happy-go-lucky, and maybe that is the best way to think of Bill Robinson. He was loved by his fans, and he made people smile. His feet really did bring joy to the world.

SECRETARIAT
(1970-1989)

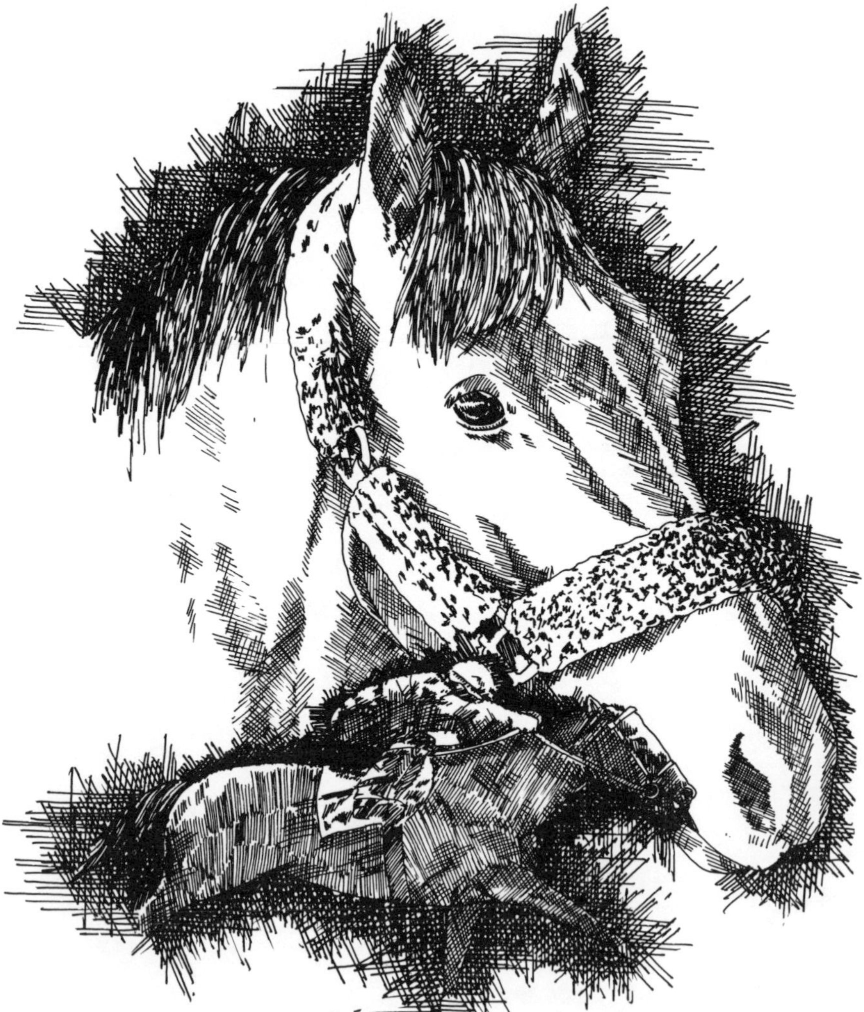

... *"superhorse"*

"SUPERHORSE." "BIG RED." Was Secretariat the greatest racehorse who ever lived? Many people think so. Certainly no horse has captured the interest and imagination of an entire country as this horse did.

Secretariat was foaled on March 20, 1970, at Meadow Stable in Doswell, Virginia. His ownership was determined by a coin toss. Each year, the owner of Meadow Stable would send two of his mares to a neighboring stable where the stud horse Bold Ruler lived. Bold Ruler had finished fourth in the 1957 Kentucky Derby. According to the arrangement, each stable would get to keep one of the foals. A coin toss determined that Meadow Stable would keep Secretariat. His mother was a horse named Somethingroyal.

The young Secretariat was a beautiful horse to behold. He had a coppery, chestnut-colored coat, and a thin white stripe that went from the top of his forehead down to the tip of his nose. Three of his legs had white markings, known as "stockings." When the owner of Meadow Stable first saw him, her reaction was simply to say, "Wow!"

Secretariat's owner and trainer had high expectations of their horses. But in his first race, Secretariat was bumped as soon as he left the starting gate. He lost that race, but he won his next seven starts. He was getting a lot of attention and was quickly mentioned as a possible entry into the Kentucky Derby. After he was named "Horse of the Year" in 1972, speculation began to grow.

The Kentucky Derby is the first of three races that make up the Triple Crown of Thoroughbred racing.

The other two important races are the Preakness in Baltimore, Maryland, and the Belmont Stakes in Elmont, New York. These races are only open to three-year-old horses, and only eight horses had ever won all three races. It had been twenty-five years since there had been a Triple Crown winner.

Secretariat's owner thought her horse could do it. Helen ("Penny") Tweedy was the daughter of Christopher Chenery, who had founded Meadow Stable in 1956. Their stable was located on the North Anna River, about twenty miles north of Richmond. In the previous year, another of their horses, Riva Ridge, had won the Kentucky Derby. Riva Ridge and Secretariat were stablemates at Meadow Stable.

Penny Tweedy had hired Lucien Laurin to train Secretariat. She also made sure that Ron Turcotte, who had been Riva Ridge's jockey, was also the jockey for Secretariat.

When Secretariat walked onto the Kentucky Derby track in Louisville, he was favored to win the race. He wore his usual blue and white checkered blinkers, and his jockey wore matching blue and white checkered silks.

In typical Secretariat style, he came out of the starting gate last, then gradually gained speed. He won the race and finished two and a half horse lengths ahead of the second place horse. He set many records that day. He ran the Kentucky Derby's one and a quarter miles in 1:59 and two-fifths of a second, a record that still stands. He ran the fastest final quarter-mile and the fastest half-mile in Derby history. In fact, he picked up speed throughout the race, running each successive quarter-mile faster than the one that had preceded it.

Later that month, he won the Preakness. Excitement was building around Secretariat. Would he be able to win the Belmont Stakes and become a Triple Crown winner? In the weeks before the race, his picture appeared on the covers of many magazines, including *Time, Newsweek,* and *Sports Illustrated.*

Secretariat was up to the challenge. He won the Belmont Stakes in a record time, finishing an amazing thirty-one horse lengths ahead of the closest horse. Secretariat was a Triple Crown winner!

Secretariat was no longer just a racehorse. He was a national hero. People wanted to touch him and be photographed with him. He raced a few more times and was then retired. But people didn't forget "Big Red." Every year, he received dozens of birthday cards and letters from his admirers. Someone once sent him a hand-hooked rug, and right in the middle was a likeness of Secretariat.

Once his racing days were over, Secretariat was highly valued as a stud horse, and his offspring were equally prized. One of his offspring was the first foal to be sold for a million dollars. Secretariat sired over 300 horses. Among them were Risen Star, who won the 1988 Preakness and Belmont Stakes, and Lady's Secret, who was the 1986 Horse of the Year.

The world was stunned to learn of Secretariat's premature death in 1989. On September 4, he contracted a painful hoof disease called laminitis, which is incurable. His owner hated the thought of having him destroyed, but she also hated to see him suffer. Secretariat had lived a wonderful life, and she decided that it would be wrong for him to live his final days in misery. On October 4, he was given a lethal injection so that he could die peacefully.

CAPT. JOHN SMITH

(1580-1631)

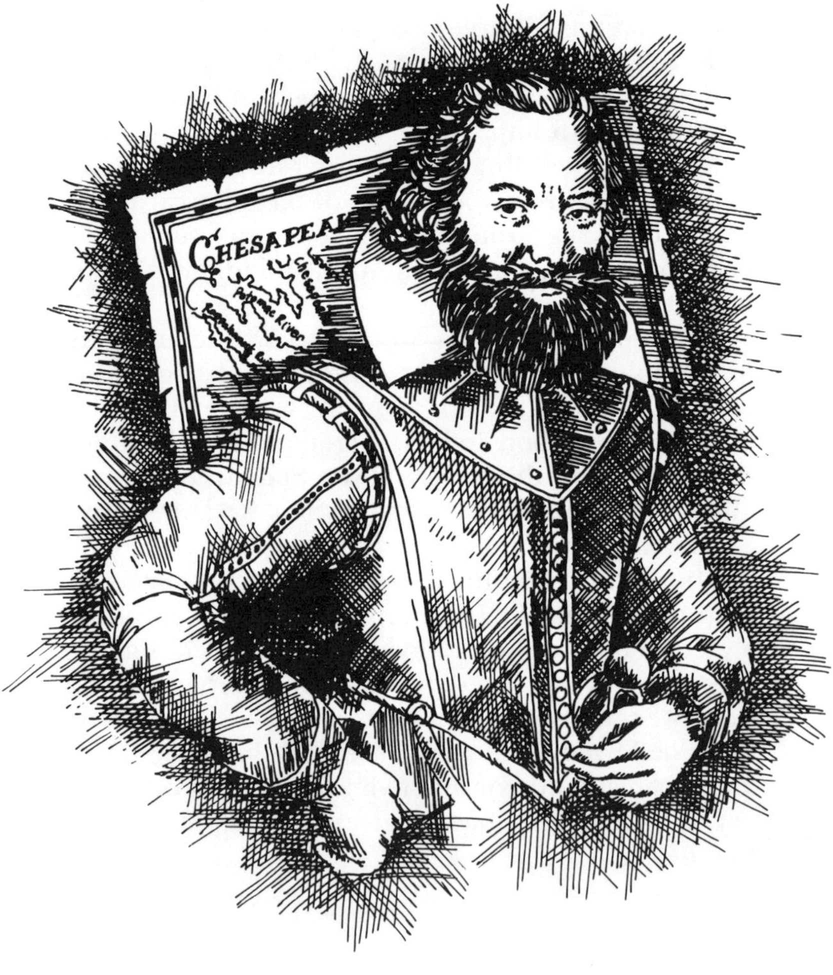
CHESAPEA
Potomac River

. . . *founder of Jamestown*

MANY PEOPLE CONTRIBUTED to England's success in exploring and settling their Virginia colony. Sir Walter Raleigh organized and helped to pay for many voyages of exploration. Powhatan, chief of the native Indians, traded food that the colonists needed desperately in order to survive. And Pocahontas befriended the colonists, converted to Christianity, and married one of the English, John Rolfe.

But Capt. John Smith, perhaps more than anyone else, helped the Jamestown colony survive. Since he had the most experience as a soldier, his knowledge helped the colonists protect themselves from the Indians, and he worked hard to establish good relations with the Indians. He was the first colonist to learn the Indian language, and he was able to trade with the Indians. Without his skills as a soldier and a negotiator, the colonists would all have been killed by the Indians, or they would have starved to death.

John Smith was born in the town of Willoughby in Lincolnshire, England, and he grew up on his family's farm. John was the oldest child, and his father wanted him to grow up to be a farmer, too. But John wanted a life of adventure. When John was a teenager, his father died and his mother remarried. For a while, John was apprenticed to a merchant, but soon he saved his money and left England for a life as a soldier.

John's life was filled with the adventure he was seeking. In his first experience as a soldier, he fought in the Dutch Army for four years against the Spanish. John then returned to England and began reading books on warfare. He dreamed of being a knight in armor. But the days of knighthood were over, since war in John's time was fought with muskets. John decided to join one of the armies that was being organized to fight the Turks, who had invaded eastern Europe.

In one of the battles, John invented a method of sending signals with torches that helped his commander send messages to the front. John was promoted to captain at the age of twenty-two. But in a later battle, the Christian soldiers were outnumbered by the Turks. Many soldiers were killed or wounded. John, too, was wounded, and taken prisoner by the Turks. They took him to a market where he was sold as a slave and sent to Turkey, where he worked as a laborer. He was treated very cruelly there, and he seized the first opportunity to escape.

John Smith was able to return to England in 1604, when he was twenty-four. For two years he planned a voyage to the English colony in Virginia. In December 1606, the group began its voyage with three ships, the *Susan Constant,* the *God Speed,* and the *Discovery.* They arrived in the Chesapeake Bay on April 26, 1607, and named their settlement Jamestown in honor of King James I of England.

Captain Smith spent much of his time exploring and mapping the Chesapeake Bay and many rivers in Virginia. He met many Indians during these explorations. At first, the Indians left the settlers alone, but later they became interested in the strange white men. Fighting began to break out between the Indians and the colonists, and on one of his scouting missions, Captain Smith was attacked by the Indians. He was shot in the leg by arrows, and taken by the Indians to their chief, Powhatan. After the elders of the tribe met, they decided that John Smith should be executed. They had large stone slabs brought to them, and they forced John to lie on them. Legend says that as they prepared to beat him to death, the chief's daughter, Pocahontas, begged her father to spare

John, and he was allowed to return to the Jamestown settlement.

Captain Smith was elected president of the Jamestown colony in 1608, and he worked to organize the settlers so they could grow more of their own food and protect themselves against the Indians.

On one night in the following year, Captain Smith and a group of men were resting on a ship after a day of exploring. One of the men accidently set on fire the gunpowder bag that Captain Smith had attached to his belt. Captain Smith was very badly burned, and he was sent home to England on the next ship. The colonists did not expect him to live. But by the time his boat arrived in England, his wounds had healed and he was able to walk off the boat without help.

After Captain Smith left Jamestown, a large number of the settlers were massacred by the Indians. But new settlers continued to arrive, and the colony survived and grew.

John Smith was not finished exploring, however. In 1614, he set off again, this time north of Jamestown to the area he named New England. He made very detailed maps of the Atlantic coastline.

On another attempt at exploring, he was captured by pirates. While on board, he began writing his description of New England. He managed to escape to France, and he returned to England. One final attempt to sail to the New World failed because strong winds kept him from leaving England.

Capt. John Smith returned to his farm in Lincolnshire, where he continued to write descriptions of the New World and his adventures with the Jamestown colony. His writings helped to encourage many others to seek their fortunes in Virginia. His maps of Virginia and New England were copied and used for many years by the explorers and settlers who followed in his footsteps to the New World.

WILLIAM STYRON
(1925-Present)

. . . *great American writer*

WILLIAM STYRON would be on almost everybody's short list of major contemporary American writers. His novels and short stories have won praise for their poetic language, and for their treatment of the themes of conflict and rebellion. William Styron has been favorably compared to other Southern writers of the twentieth century, most notably the great William Faulkner.

The plots and themes of William Styron's works have been largely influenced by the South, and by the experiences of his youth. He was born in Newport News, Virginia, where his father, who had English ancestors, worked as a marine engineer. William's mother died when he was thirteen, at about the same time that he began attending Christchurch Preparatory School in Middlesex County, Virginia. William wanted to be an engineer like his father. But while he was away at school, he wrote articles for the school paper.

William continued to write after he began college, first at Davidson College and then at Duke University in North Carolina. While he was at Duke, he was encouraged to write short stories. Some of them were published in Duke University's literary magazine.

William served in the Marine Corps for three years as a guard at a naval prison, and he worked briefly at the McGraw-Hill book publishing company.

William Styron began working on his first novel, *Lie Down in Darkness*, in 1948, and it was published three years later. It tells the story of a respectable family that is torn apart by the death of their adult daughter. The story is told in the form of flashbacks from the funeral.

His next works, *The Long March* and *Set This House on Fire,* were published in the next ten years. William Styron became a fellow at Silliman College of Yale University in 1964. And in 1967 he published his most acclaimed novel, *The Confessions of Nat Turner.* It won the Pulitzer Prize in 1968.

The Confessions of Nat Turner is a fictionalized account of a real event, the slave revolt led by Nat Turner in 1831. William Styron grew up near Southampton, where Nat Turner's revolt occurred.

Nat Turner was a slave who was a servant to a kind white master. Nat was also a preacher, and he had a vision in which God told him to murder the white slaveholders. Nat and about sixty of his followers went on a rampage, killing about fifty-five white persons in the area. Eventually, Nat and his followers were captured and hanged. And, as a result of the revolt, many slaveholders became scared and were more strict with their slaves. Some people believe that this crackdown on the slaves helped to make the Civil War happen sooner than it might have otherwise occurred.

The Confessions of Nat Turner tells the story of the revolt from Nat Turner's point of view. Some people criticized William Styron for writing the book. Some black people felt that, as a white man, he had no right to tell this story. Some white people believed that the book was bad for relations between black and white people. But William Styron believed that the story of Nat Turner was an important one to tell. At the time the book was published, the civil rights movement in America was at its height. People needed to know about the history of slavery, and to understand the reasons why black people demanded their rights.

In 1979, William Styron published another novel, *Sophie's Choice.* It is the story of an aspiring young writer from the South who becomes friends with Sophie, a woman who has survived the Nazi death camps of World War II. Although she survived the war, her two small children did not. The story of her war experiences and her life after the war is surely one of the saddest stories in all of American fiction.

William Styron's contributions to American literature are greater than the stories of his characters' struggles with crisis. The richness of his language and the very poetry of his writing make him an important author for all time.

BOOKER T. WASHINGTON
(1856-1915)

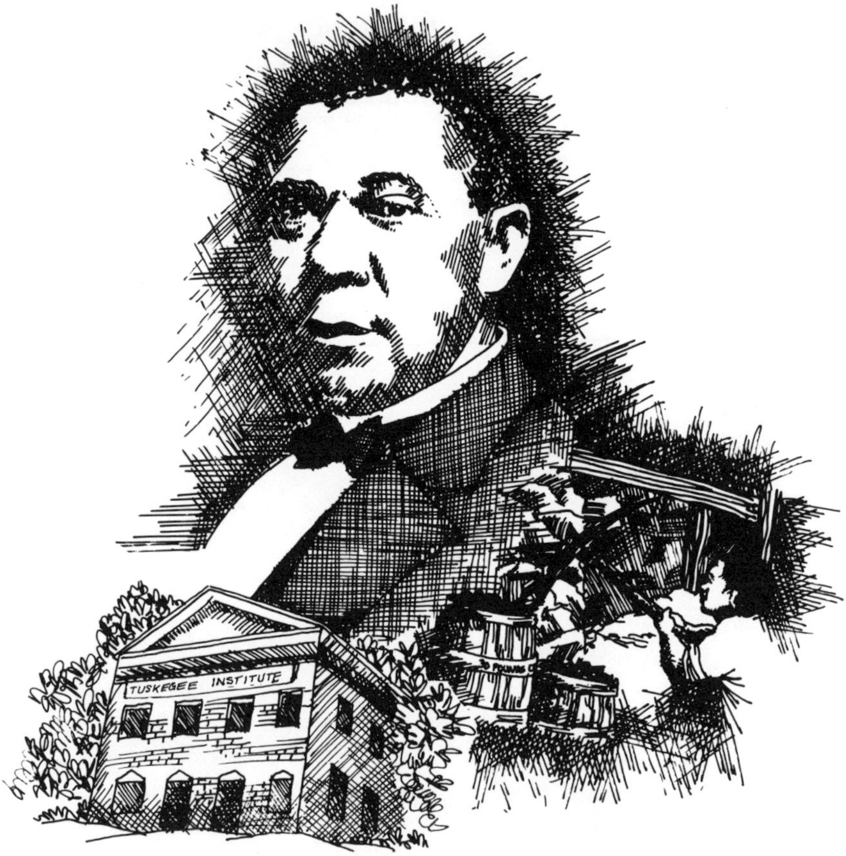
TUSKEGEE INSTITUTE

...from slave to educator

FOR THE LAST twenty years of his life, Booker T. Washington was the most powerful and influential black person in America. He met with presidents, ate dinner at the White House with Pres. Theodore Roosevelt, and had tea in London with Queen Victoria. He was the first black person to receive an honorary degree from Harvard University. Yet all of his honors and accomplishments were earned in spite of his being born a slave, in the worst poverty imaginable.

Booker T. Washington was born into slavery in a small log cabin in Franklin County, Virginia. (His birthplace is now a historic site in Rocky Mount, Virginia.) His mother was the cook for the owners of the plantation. Little Booker never even knew the name of his father.

Freedom came when Booker was nine years old, and the family moved to Malden, West Virginia, where his stepfather was working. Booker went to work, first in a salt furnace, then in a coal mine. It was hard, tiring work. But Booker was expected to do his share.

In the mines, Booker saw strange markings on the sides of barrels. He learned that these markings were numbers, and he became determined to learn how to read. Sometimes a black person who could read or write would pass through town, and Booker and others would try to learn all they could. But after a while, the black people realized that they needed to organize. They started a school for themselves, and many times the school was taught by the only person who knew how to read or write. The people who worked in the mines would attend school in the evenings, and children and adults would sit side by side as they learned.

One day, while Booker worked in the mine, he overheard two people talking about a school for blacks in Hampton, Virginia. Booker was determined to go there. At first, his family was against it, since they needed him at home. Finally, they gave their consent. Booker was only sixteen, but he travelled over 500 miles to Hampton by himself, partly by train, and the rest on foot. When he arrived there, he had no money, so he worked as a janitor in order to earn his keep.

While he was at the Hampton Normal and Agricultural Institute, Booker met Gen. Samuel C. Armstrong. General Armstrong was a Northerner who wanted to help blacks learn and get ahead. He inspired Booker to work hard and learn. After Booker graduated from Hampton three years later, he returned to Malden and taught in the local school. But in a few years, General Armstrong hired Booker to return to Hampton as a teacher. In addition to teaching, Booker supervised seventy-five Indian students and ran a night school for poor students.

In 1881, some people in Alabama asked General Armstrong to recommend a principal for a new school that they were starting for blacks. They expected that General Armstrong would recommend a white man, but he suggested Booker T. Washington.

Before he left Hampton, he had never heard of Tuskegee, Alabama. But Booker T. Washington was determined to make the school a success. When he arrived, Washington was only twenty-five years old. He soon discovered that the only school buildings were a shack and a church. Instead of being discouraged, he worked to raise money for the school, and he borrowed money from friends at Hampton to buy an abandoned plantation.

Tuskegee Normal and Agricultural Institute was not a liberal arts college. Booker T. Washington believed that blacks needed industrial training so that they could earn their places in society. So, the students were expected to work hard, as part of their education. Most of the new school buildings were built by student labor. The students built their own furniture, and they took care of crops and livestock. They cooked and cleaned, and did their own laundry. By learning practical skills, Booker believed that blacks could earn economic equality with whites, which would then lead to full equality and justice under the law.

Booker T. Washington travelled across the country to raise funds for Tuskegee. He received the support of both philanthropists and average citizens who were concerned about the future of black people in the South. In time, Tuskegee Institute gained a national reputation, and Booker became a well-known speaker on education and the future of black people.

In 1895, Booker T. Washington made a famous speech in Atlanta at the Cotton States and International Exhibition. It was the first major address given in the South by a black man to a racially mixed audience. He said, "In all things that are purely social we can be as separate as the fingers, yet one as the hand in all things essential to mutual progress." He went on to say that when blacks educated themselves, they would find that their trades and professions would be recognized regardless of their race. Booker became the first black American who had the approval and support of large numbers of both whites and blacks.

He wrote several books, including *Up from Slavery*, his most famous, which tells the story of his youth and the founding of Tuskegee Institute.

Although he remained very popular, a younger generation of blacks criticized him for not demanding total, immediate equality. Nevertheless, they could not challenge his accomplishments. When Booker T. Washington died in 1915, Tuskegee Institute had over sixty buildings and had graduated thousands of students. His legacy lives on to this day at Tuskegee Institute, which continues to educate a new generation of black students.

GEORGE WASHINGTON
(1732-1799)

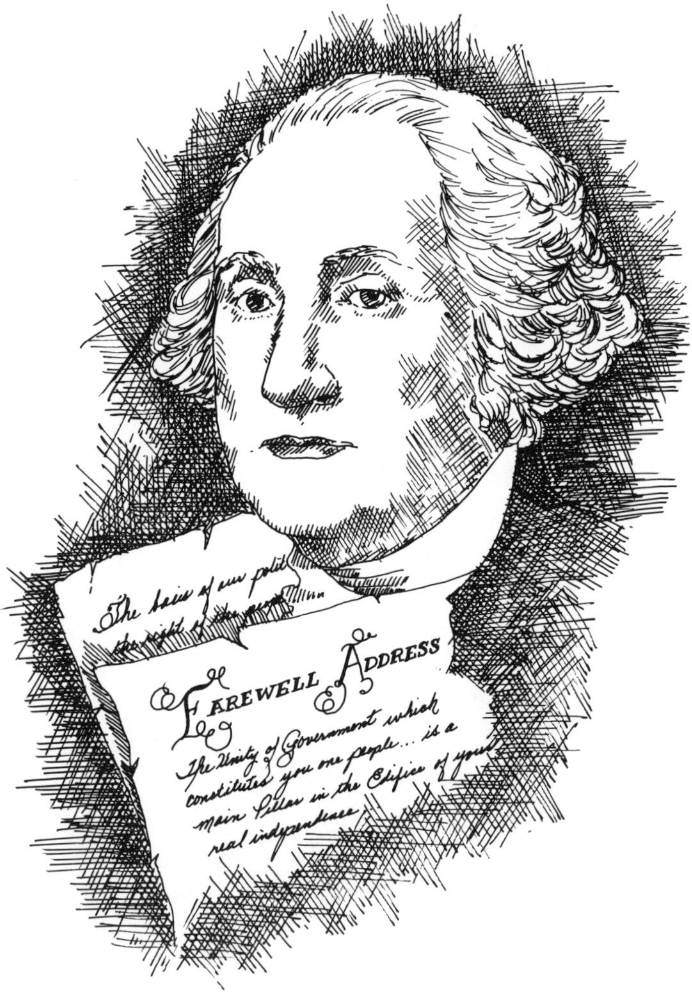
FAREWELL ADDRESS
The Unity of Government which
constitutes you one people... is a
main Pillar in the Edifice of your
real independence

. . . first in the hearts of his countrymen

WHEN WE THINK of George Washington, we usually think of him in very simple terms. He was the first president of the United States. He was a Revolutionary War hero. And when we try to picture him, we see only the stern face of a man from 200 years ago, wearing a powdered wig and clothes that look foreign to us. These thoughts and images of George Washington are not incorrect, but they only begin to describe the living, breathing man that was George Washington.

George Washington was a Southern gentleman and a planter, more comfortable at Mount Vernon tending his estate than he was in leading an army or his country. But he knew that his countrymen needed him, and he always responded to their call.

His family were land owners from England, but they were not especially prosperous. His father, Augustine Washington, had been a member of the House of Burgesses. George and his family moved several times during his youth in search of more fertile farmland. George's father had two sons from his first marriage, but George was the oldest child of Augustine and Mary Ball Washington.

George was born on his father's estate at Pope's Creek in Westmoreland County near Wakefield, Virginia. The Washington family eventually settled at the Ferry Farm on the Rappahannock River, after first moving to the Hunting Creek plantation on the present site of Mount Vernon.

When George was young, his father died. After helping his mother run the farm for a few years, George wanted to leave for a life at sea. He had been excited by stories of adventure, and he especially wanted to visit London. But his mother and older brother talked him into staying behind to manage the family estate. They convinced him that he could join the militia and have an exciting life in Virginia.

George's older half-brother, Lawrence, married a daughter of the wealthy Fairfax family. Soon, George was invited to join in many of their family's activities. Lawrence had inherited the Mount Vernon house, and George enjoyed spending time there with his brother.

George grew up to be a tall, strong young man. He was six feet, two and a half inches tall, and he was known to be a good wrestler and an excellent horseman. He was intelligent in spite of having had little formal education. He took an interest in surveying when the Fairfax family invited him to join a party of men who travelled to survey their lands in the West. When he was seventeen, George was appointed to be the surveyor of Culpeper County, Virginia, and he helped to plan the new city of Alexandria, north of Mount Vernon.

His brother Lawrence became sick with tuberculosis, and he and George travelled to Barbados in an effort to work a cure. There, George contracted a mild case of smallpox, which scarred his face. Lawrence died after their return to Virginia, and the Mount Vernon estate soon passed to George's possession.

In 1753, when he was twenty-one, George Washington was appointed to be a major in the militia. He fought in the French and Indian War and observed the strength of the French Army. He served under General Braddock in the fighting against the French, and in 1755 he was made a colonel and was chosen to command the entire Virginia militia.

George Washington married Martha Dandridge Custis in 1759. She was a wealthy widow with two small children, and they lived briefly in Williamsburg while George was a member of the House of Burgesses. Soon they moved to Mount Vernon and began taking care of their large estate. Mount Vernon was almost like a small town. There were several hundred slaves on the estate, and all kinds of tradesmen for taking care of their needs. They produced most of their own food, clothing, and other necessities.

George Washington continued to serve in the House of Burgesses, and he gained respect as a person who could work out compromises between people with different opinions. But, in time, many of the people in Virginia and the other colonies began to resent the way that the British governed them. They were especially upset by heavy taxes that the British imposed on them, without their approval or consent. In 1774, George Washington was elected as a delegate from Virginia to the First Constitutional Congress in Philadelphia.

Conditions in the colonies worsened, and fighting broke out in 1775 between the colonies and the British Army. George Washington attended the Second Continental Congress, where he was elected general of the Continental Army. At that time, the Continental Army was no more than loosely organized armies of state militiamen, and sometimes they fought among themselves. George realized that his first mission was to organize and inspire the troops.

The Revolutionary War lasted many years, and it was not always clear which side would win. The Continental Army defeated the British in Boston, Trenton, Princeton, and Saratoga, but Washington's men also lost several battles. Many Continental Army soldiers died during the long, cold winter at Valley Forge, Pennsylvania. But Washington's troops surrounded and defeated the British Army at Yorktown, Virginia in 1781, and news of the British surrender reached the colonies in 1783. Washington resigned from the Army and returned to Mount Vernon. He enjoyed tending his fields, and he bred horses and hunting dogs.

In 1787, Washington presided at the Constitutional Convention in Philadelphia and worked hard to ensure that all the states would ratify the constitution. The Congress unanimously chose George Washington to be the first president of the United States, and he took the oath as president in New York in 1789. He served for a total of eight years.

While he was president, Washington encouraged people to explore and settle in the western territories. During his term in office, Vermont, Tennessee, and Kentucky joined the thirteen original states in the union. George Washington also supported the move of the nation's capital to a new city on the Potomac River, that would become Washington, D.C.

George Washington died at Mount Vernon in 1799 after a brief illness. Upon his death, it was said, "First in war, first in peace, and first in the hearts of his countrymen, he was second to none in the humble and endearing scenes of private life."

MARTHA WASHINGTON
(1732-1802)

... the first First Lady

MARTHA DANDRIDGE was something of a tomboy. More than anything else, she loved riding her horse across her family's plantation in Virginia. Her father, John Dandridge, was a successful English tobacco farmer and a county clerk, as well as a colonel in the militia. Perhaps he favored his daughter over his other children because she was so much like him—lively and free-spirited.

Martha Dandridge was born on her parents' Chestnut Grove plantation in 1732. Chestnut Grove was located about twenty-five miles from Williamsburg on the Pamunkey River, which is a fork of the York River.

Almost immediately after Martha was born, her father nicknamed her "Patsy," and it was by this name that she was known. Like most girls of her day, she received no formal education. But when her mother heard that a tutor was settling in the area, she arranged for him to tutor all her children. He taught the children reading, writing, and some arithmetic.

When she was fifteen, Martha's life changed forever and she put her childhood behind her. Each year, the young women of well-to-do families were presented at the annual Governor's Ball in Williamsburg. Many of the young women came to the ball dressed in fine gowns from England, but Martha appeared in a homemade gown. Even so, she attracted the attention of Daniel Parke Custis, who was the son of the planter John Custis, one of the wealthiest men in Virginia. Daniel Parke Custis was twenty years older than Martha Dandridge, but he began courting her and would have married her sooner than he did. However, his father was opposed to his son marrying Martha, because he did not think highly of her family. Two years went by and finally, Martha met John Custis by accident. He was so charmed by the young Martha that he changed his mind and consented to the marriage. Martha and Daniel were married in 1749, when Martha was only seventeen.

Martha and Daniel Custis had a happy marriage. They lived at The White House, which was the name of the Custis family's plantation on the Pamunkey River in New Kent County. They had four children, Daniel and Frances (who both died as children), then John and Martha (who were known as Jacky and Patsy).

Once, when Martha and Daniel were at a ball in Fredericksburg, they happened to meet Col. George Washington. He was a hero of the French and Indian War, and he had fought at the side of General Braddock. Both Martha and Daniel were very impressed by Colonel Washington.

In 1757, Daniel Custis died after a brief illness, leaving Martha to take care of their two small children. She was only twenty-five years old at the time. But she inherited The White House and all of Daniel's property, and she became one of the wealthiest women in Virginia.

Six months after Daniel Custis died, Martha once again met George Washington, this time at a friend's house. He had grown disillusioned about his career, and she was still in mourning. But they found comfort in each other's company. They were married on January 6, 1759, at The White House, only eighteen months after Daniel Custis died. Their wedding was attended by Governor Fauquier and many other prominent Virginians.

By Virginia law, all of Martha's property now belonged to her new husband. She moved into George

Washington's house at Mount Vernon. At that time, Mount Vernon was a simple eight-room house, but George and Martha lived the lives of wealthy planters. George served his native state as a representative in the House of Burgesses in Williamsburg.

Their lives might have continued in this relative peace, but in the 1770s, trouble was brewing in the colonies. The British Parliament in London passed new taxes on tea, paint, and other essential items that the colonists had to import from England. George Washington attended the Continental Congress, and when the thirteen colonies declared their independence from Great Britain, he was chosen to lead the Continental Army.

Once again, Martha Washington's life would never be the same. George Washington was a loving father to Martha's two surviving children, but then Patsy died, leaving only Jacky. He married and had four children, and Martha helped raise them. Jacky left Mount Vernon to join his stepfather in the war, but he died of trench fever. (One of Jacky's granddaughters would later marry Robert E. Lee.)

Martha Washington joined her husband and the Continental Army during the winter months when fighting was at a low point. She was in Valley Forge, Pennsylvania, during the harshest, coldest winter months of the Revolutionary War.

After the British surrendered at Yorktown, Virginia, in 1781, the Washingtons wanted nothing more than to return to their simple lives at Mount Vernon. But the new United States of America had other work for them. George Washington worked on the U.S. Constitution in Philadelphia in 1787, and a year later he was elected the nation's first president. The Washingtons left Mount Vernon for New York, the nation's first capital, where George was inaugurated.

Martha became known as a gracious hostess, entertaining visitors in both New York and Philadelphia. After eight years as the first First Lady, Martha Dandridge Custis Washington was able to return at last to her beloved Virginia in 1797.

Two years later, George Washington died and was buried at Mount Vernon. Martha Washington burned all their letters to each other, so that not a single letter of Martha's to her husband survives. We can only imagine the content of those letters, and suppose that she offered encouragement to her husband during the Revolutionary War and during the Continental Congress.

When Martha Washington died in 1802, she was buried next to George Washington in the family vault at Mount Vernon. Their home now welcomes thousands of visitors each year from across the country and around the world.

DOUG WILDER

(1931-Present)

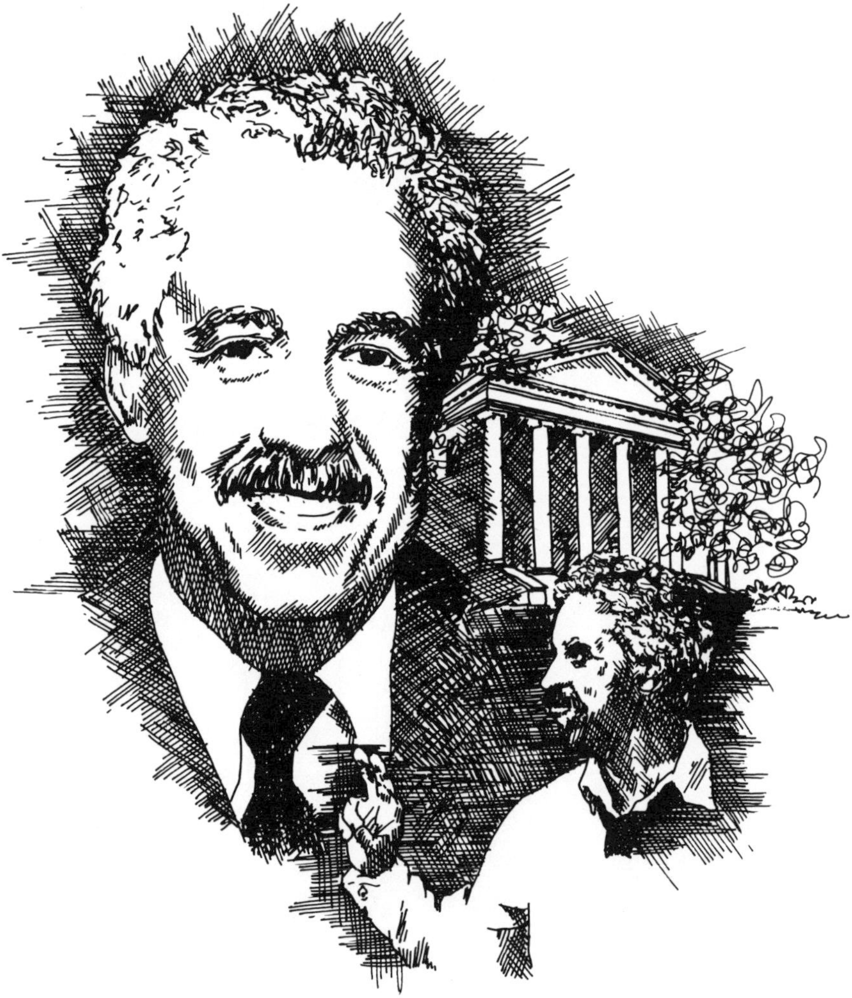

. . . pioneering governor

DOUG WILDER'S RISE from the segregated Richmond of his youth to the governor's mansion was as impressive as any Hollywood rags-to-riches story. Born the grandson of slaves, Lawrence Douglas ("Doug") Wilder grew up in the all-black Church Hill section of East Richmond. Few opportunities existed in Doug's youth, since blacks were denied access to the better schools and jobs.

But Doug Wilder knew that in spite of these obstacles, he could not take the easy road in life. His parents had taught him the importance of working hard. Robert and Beulah Wilder had high expectations for all of their eight children. The Wilders were a close-knit family, and Douglas, the youngest child, grew up in a wide circle of family, friends, and neighbors. The Wilder children heard stories of how their grandparents had been separated by the cruelty of slavery. When their grandmother was sold to a nearby plantation, their grandfather would travel every weekend to visit her and their children. The message was clear to the Wilder children: life may be difficult, but you can overcome your difficulties if you work hard enough.

The Wilder family was used to hard work. Doug's father, Robert Wilder, had a brother who studied to become a doctor. With such a goal, the whole family worked hard and sacrificed to help him with his dream. Although he eventually became a doctor, he died soon afterwards, and the family felt their loss for many years.

But in spite of their setback, Doug's parents knew that a good education was necessary for their children to succeed. Doug's mother, Beulah, taught him new words every day and worked crossword puzzles with him. The Wilder family had teas where each child was expected to perform in some way, and Doug would recite poetry that he had memorized.

The Wilder parents were strict with their children, and the children were expected to do their share of the work at home. As a youth, Doug earned money by shining shoes, washing windows, painting houses, and, later, operating an elevator.

After high school, Doug wanted to join the service, but since he was underage, he needed his parents' approval. They would not sign the papers, so Doug went to college at Virginia Union University. He worked his way through college as a waiter at the Hotel John Marshall and the William Byrd Hotel in Richmond. Since his ambition was to be an oral surgeon, Doug majored in chemistry at college. But, soon after his graduation, he was drafted into the Army and sent to fight in the Korean War.

It was years after Doug returned home from Korea that his closest friends and family learned the truth about Doug's Army service record. He and two other soldiers captured nineteen enemy prisoners on Pork Chop Hill, the scene of some of the bloodiest fighting in the war. Doug was awarded the Bronze Star for his bravery.

But when Doug returned home, he found that his college degree and his war record did not mean that he could get a good job. He was lucky to get a job as a laboratory assistant, but after working a short while on a master's degree in chemistry, he decided that he wanted to be a lawyer. He believed that by being a lawyer, he could help black people win their rights to equal treatment and equal opportunity for education and jobs.

Since the state of Virginia did not want to accept blacks into their law schools, it paid Doug to go to law school at Howard University in Washington, D.C. While he was there, he met and married Eunice Montgomery, who was an economics major.

After he graduated from law school, the Wilders moved to Richmond. Doug Wilder opened a small law office near his parents' home and took on a variety of small cases. Gradually, his reputation grew, and he began handling more important cases. He was known to be an excellent courtroom speaker, and he credits all the times that he memorized and recited poetry as a youth.

As a young lawyer, Doug Wilder took the case of a black friend who was arrested for sitting in a bus station waiting room that was reserved for white people only. Eventually, this case was decided in his friend's favor by the U.S. Supreme Court. The ruling ended segregation in waiting rooms across the South.

In 1969, Doug Wilder ran successfully as a Democrat for the Virginia State Senate, winning almost half of the votes in a three-way race. As the Senate's only black member, he pushed for fair housing laws, and for a state holiday honoring the birth of Dr. Martin Luther King, Jr.

After sixteen years in the State Senate, Doug Wilder decided to run for lieutenant governor of Virginia. The political experts gave him almost no chance of winning. But he campaigned across the state from town to town, and he convinced people that he was the best person for the job. He surprised many people by winning in a state-wide election in 1985.

Four years later, when Governor Baliles' term was coming to an end, no one was surprised when Doug Wilder announced that he was running for governor. During his campaign, he spoke out in favor of the death penalty for drug pushers, and for women's right to abortions. Doug told his audiences that the election wasn't about race, it was about improving the quality of life for all Virginians. That would mean better schools, more jobs, and controlling the state's finances. And his message got across.

In November 1989, Doug Wilder became the first elected black governor in U.S. history. Many people did not think that Virginia, the home of the Confederacy, would be the first state to elect a black person as governor. But Doug proved them wrong, again.

In a few years, Doug Wilder may be ready to make a solid bid for the U.S. Senate, the vice-presidency, or maybe even the presidency. If he chooses to pursue a national office, many people will be surprised, and a few experts will surely say that he has no chance of winning. But the people of Virginia know that Doug Wilder has beaten the odds many times already.

WOODROW WILSON
(1856-1924)

... president and Nobel Peace Prize winner

THOMAS WOODROW WILSON grew up in the South during the years of the Civil War. Unlike many boys and girls today who read about war or who see it on the television news, he knew it firsthand. He heard about and saw the Confederate soldiers who went off to war, and he heard about the terrible battles. He saw the Union prisoners of war who were held captive. And he saw the destruction that the war brought upon the people and the landscape of the South. Perhaps that is why, years later as president, he worked so hard to keep America out of war.

Thomas Woodrow Wilson was born into an Irish and Scottish family in Staunton, Virginia. (He began to be known by his middle name of Woodrow when he grew up.) He had two older sisters and a younger brother, but the biggest influence on him was his father, the Reverend Joseph Ruggles Wilson. The Reverend Wilson was a popular Presbyterian minister. Because of the Reverend Wilson's assignments, the Wilson family moved several times, to such places as Augusta, Georgia; Columbia, South Carolina; and Wilmington, North Carolina.

Tommy Wilson heard his father preach, and he was impressed by his father's ability to use his speech so effectively. Tommy thought that he wanted to be a minister, too, just like his father.

When he went to college, he joined debating clubs and discovered an interest in history and politics. He soon realized that his true calling was the law. He envisioned himself making grand speeches before courts.

He graduated from Princeton University, then returned to Virginia to study law at the University of Virginia.

In his second year, though, poor health forced him to leave law school. Woodrow (as he was now known) was to be plagued by poor health, off and on, for the rest of his life. He could, and did, work so hard and so singlemindedly on a task that he would literally wear himself out.

When he recovered, he tried to practice law with a friend in Atlanta, but he soon realized that he was more comfortable in a university setting. So, he entered Johns Hopkins University in Baltimore and earned a Ph.D. in 1886. In that same year, he married Ellen Louise Axson of Savannah, Georgia, whom he had met while in Atlanta. He taught for a while at Bryn Mawr College in Pennsylvania, and then at Wesleyan University in Connecticut. He was a popular and well-liked professor of history and political economy, and he started to be recognized as a brilliant speaker.

In 1890, his alma mater, Princeton University, offered him a position as professor of jurisprudence. He taught at Princeton for twelve years, all the while becoming more and more popular and respected. He wanted to turn Princeton into a first-rate university, and in 1902 he became its president. Almost immediately, he raised the entrance standards for the university, improved the curriculum, and hired more teachers. He tried to make the university a true place for learning and less of a social club. Although he continued to be very successful, he had his critics. Some of the other professors felt that he was changing too many things.

While he was president of Princeton University, Woodrow Wilson spoke out on political issues of the day and attracted a national following with his dynamic speeches and his progressive views. In 1910, he was offered the Democratic nomination for governor of New Jersey. After winning the election and serving as governor for only two years, he became the Democratic nominee for president of the United States. He won the election, but soon he faced both personal and political crises.

During his first term in the White House, Woodrow Wilson succeeded in pushing legislation through the Congress that promoted free trade, and helped to create the Federal Reserve Board. He also worked to have laws passed so that the people could directly elect their own U.S. senators.

In 1914, Woodrow Wilson suffered a great personal loss when his wife died. His personal losses were made even more difficult with the international struggles that threatened to pull the United States into war.

Woodrow Wilson respected the rights of other nations, and he believed in diplomacy over force. But a civil war in Mexico began to affect the United States when American border towns were raided by Pancho Villa, one of the rebel leaders. Woodrow dispatched troops to Mexico and ensured the safety of American citizens.

Wilson remarried while president, and he was happy again. But soon, another crisis faced him. War had broken out in Europe.

The alliance of England and France was under attack by the German empire. Woodrow Wilson tried desperately to keep the United States out of the war. At this time, the United States was not considered to be a major world power. It did not have a large standing army, and its navy was not that powerful. Germany stepped up its war against the Allies by using its submarines to sink cargo vessels and the passenger liner *Lusitania,* killing American citizens. Woodrow protested and threatened to end diplomatic relations with Germany. He wanted the United States to remain neutral in the war.

For a while, Wilson's threats seemed to work. He was narrowly reelected president in 1916 on a platform of continued neutrality, and his campaign slogan was "He kept us out of war." Most Americans at that time believed that the United States needed to take care of its own problems, and not meddle in other countries' business.

A few months after the election, the Germans renewed their submarine war, and they would not promise to stop sinking passenger ships. The American people finally concluded that they had to join the European war effort in order to protect themselves. In March 1917, the U.S. Congress declared war.

The American involvement in World War I ended in November 1918, with the German surrender. Woodrow Wilson travelled to Paris to personally negotiate a treaty to end the war, and to secure the peace.

Woodrow Wilson was interested in more than ending the war. He wanted a way to keep the peace, through the cooperation of all nations against aggression. He proposed a League of Nations that would respond as a united force if any member was attacked.

Most countries agreed to this approach, but the U.S. Congress would not give their consent to this treaty. They did not want the United States to fight every time someone else needed help.

Woodrow Wilson decided to take his case directly to the American people. He started a cross-country speaking tour by train, giving two or three major speeches every day, to rally support for his League of Nations. While in Colorado, he suffered a stroke and was forced to end his speaking tour and return to Washington.

His health gradually returned, but Woodrow Wilson was never again a well man. Although he did not run for reelection in 1920, he was awarded the Nobel Peace Prize for his efforts to negotiate an end to the war. He lived in Washington, D.C., until his death in 1924.

No one will ever know if America's participation in the League of Nations could have averted World War II. But the United Nations, which was formed after World War II, was created on the same principles that Woodrow Wilson had fought for thirty years earlier.